Benefits for Students in Scotland Handbook

17th edition

Angela Toal

Child Poverty Action Group in Scotland

Child Poverty Action Group works on behalf of the more than one in four children in the UK growing up in poverty. It does not have to be like this. We use our understanding of what causes poverty and the impact it has on children's lives to campaign for policies that will prevent and solve poverty – for good. We provide training, advice and information to make sure hard-up families get the financial support they need. We also carry out high-profile legal work to establish and protect families' rights. If you are not already supporting us, please consider making a donation, or ask for details of our membership schemes, training courses and publications.

Published by Child Poverty Action Group
30 Micawber Street
London N1 7TB
Tel: 020 7837 7979
staff@cpag.org.uk
www.cpag.org.uk

© Child Poverty Action Group 2019

This book is sold subject to the condition that it shall not, by way of trade or otherwise, be lent, resold, hired out or otherwise circulated without the publisher's prior consent in any form of binding or cover other than that in which it is published and without a similar condition including this condition being imposed on the subsequent purchaser.

A CIP record for this book is available from the British Library.

ISBN: 978 1 910715 58 1

Child Poverty Action Group is a charity registered in England and Wales (registration number 294841) and in Scotland (registration number SC039339), and is a company limited by guarantee, registered in England (registration number 1993854). VAT number: 690 808117.

Cover design by Colorido Studios
Internal design by Devious Designs
Typeset by DLxml, a division of RefineCatch Limited, Bungay, Suffolk
Content management system by Konnect Soft
Printed and bound by CPI Group (UK) Ltd, Croydon CR0 4YY

The author

Angela Toal is a welfare rights worker with CPAG in Scotland, working on its Benefits for Students Project.

Acknowledgements

First and foremost, many thanks to Judith Paterson, Head of Advice and Rights at CPAG in Scotland, who wrote the first few editions of this *Handbook* and continues to provide invaluable checking and advice. Many thanks also to Gwyneth King at CPAG in Scotland for checking this edition.

Grateful thanks are due to staff at the Student Awards Agency Scotland and the Scottish Funding Council for their time and expertise in checking and advising on this *Handbook*. Thanks too to all of those on the project advisory group for their support and encouragement throughout the year.

Many thanks go to John Dickie and everyone else at CPAG in Scotland for their invaluable support and practical help.

Many thanks also to Alison Key for editing and managing the production of the book, Anne Ketley for compiling the index and Kathleen Armstrong for proofreading the text.

CPAG is grateful for the Scottish government's financial support towards this *Handbook*.

Contents

Abbreviations	x
Means-tested benefit rates 2019/20	xi
Non-means-tested benefit rates 2019/20	xv
Tax credit rates 2019/20	xvii
How to use this *Handbook*	xviii
Benefits and tax credits: overview	xx

Part 1 Benefits and tax credits

Chapter 1 Carer's allowance	3
1. What is carer's allowance	3
2. Who is eligible	4
3. Amount of benefit	5
4. Claiming carer's allowance	5
5. Challenging a decision	5
6. Other benefits and tax credits	6
Chapter 2 Child benefit	8
1. What is child benefit	8
2. Who is eligible	8
3. Amount of benefit	12
4. Claiming child benefit	12
5. Challenging a decision	12
6. Other benefits and tax credits	13
Chapter 3 Disability living allowance	14
1. What is disability living allowance	14
2. Who is eligible	15
3. Amount of benefit	18
4. Claiming disability living allowance	18
5. Challenging a decision	18
6. Other benefits and tax credits	19
Chapter 4 Employment and support allowance	20
1. What is employment and support allowance	20
2. Who is eligible	21
3. Limited capability for work	23
4. Amount of benefit	24

5. Claiming employment and support allowance	29
6. Challenging a decision	29
7. Other benefits and tax credits	29

Chapter 5   Health benefits — 31
1. What are health benefits — 31
2. Who is eligible — 31
3. Claiming health benefits — 35
4. Challenging a decision — 36

Chapter 6   Housing benefit — 37
1. What is housing benefit — 37
2. Who is eligible — 38
3. Basic rules — 40
4. Amount of benefit — 43
5. Claiming housing benefit — 48
6. Challenging a decision — 48
7. Other benefits and tax credits — 49

Chapter 7   Income support — 51
1. What is income support — 51
2. Who is eligible — 52
3. Basic rules — 60
4. Amount of benefit — 60
5. Claiming income support — 64
6. Challenging a decision — 65
7. Other benefits and tax credits — 65

Chapter 8   Jobseeker's allowance — 68
1. What is jobseeker's allowance — 68
2. Who is eligible — 69
3. Basic rules — 74
4. Amount of benefit — 75
5. Claiming jobseeker's allowance — 77
6. Challenging a decision — 77
7. Other benefits and tax credits — 78

Chapter 9   Maternity, paternity and adoption benefits — 80
1. What are maternity, paternity and adoption benefits — 80
2. Who is eligible — 81
3. Amount of benefit — 83
4. Claiming maternity, paternity and adoption benefits — 83

5. Challenging a decision	83
6. Other benefits and tax credits	84

Chapter 10 Personal independence payment — 85
1. What is personal independence payment — 85
2. Who is eligible — 86
3. Amount of benefit — 87
4. Claiming personal independence payment — 87
5. Challenging a decision — 88
6. Other benefits and tax credits — 88

Chapter 11 Universal credit — 89
1. What is universal credit — 89
2. Who is eligible — 90
3. Basic rules — 93
4. Amount of benefit — 93
5. Claiming universal credit — 97
6. Challenging a decision — 98
7. Other benefits and tax credits — 98

Chapter 12 Child tax credit — 101
1. What is child tax credit — 101
2. Who is eligible — 102
3. Amount of child tax credit — 103
4. Claiming child tax credit — 105
5. Challenging a decision — 106
6. Tax credits and benefits — 106

Chapter 13 Working tax credit — 108
1. What is working tax credit — 108
2. Who is eligible — 109
3. Amount of working tax credit — 110
4. Claiming working tax credit — 112
5. Challenging a decision — 113
6. Tax credits and benefits — 113

Chapter 14 Other payments — 114
1. Best Start grants — 114
2. Best Start foods — 115
3. Funeral support payments — 115
4. Budgeting loans — 116
5. The Scottish Welfare Fund — 116
6. Challenging a decision — 117

Part 2 **Student support**	
Chapter 15 Student support	121
1. Full-time higher education	121
2. Full-time further education	124
3. Part-time students	127
4. Postgraduates	128
5. Nursing and midwifery students	128
6. Other support for students	129
Part 3 **Treatment of income**	
Chapter 16 How income affects universal credit	133
1. Working out your income	133
2. Grants and loans	134
3. Dividing income throughout the year	136
4. Other payments	137
5. Earnings	137
6. Benefits	138
7. Maintenance	138
8. Savings and other capital	138
Chapter 17 How income affects means-tested benefits	140
1. Working out your income	141
2. Grants and loans	142
3. Dividing student income throughout the year	146
4. Discretionary funds and other payments	153
5. Earnings	155
6. Benefits and tax credits	156
7. Maintenance	156
8. Savings and other capital	157
Chapter 18 How income affects tax credits	160
1. Working out your income	160
2. Grants and loans	162
3. Earnings	163
4. Benefits	163
5. Other income	164
Chapter 19 How income affects health benefits	166
1. Working out your income	166
2. Grants and loans	167
3. Discretionary funds and other payments	169
4. Earnings	170
5. Benefits and tax credits	170

6. Maintenance	171
7. Savings and other capital	171

Part 4 Other matters

Chapter 20 Council tax	175
1. What is council tax	175
2. Who pays council tax	176
3. Council tax reduction	180
4. Second adult rebate	181
Chapter 21 Time out from studies	184
1. Ill health	187
2. Pregnancy and children	187
3. Carers	188
4. Re-sits	188
5. Time out for other reasons	188

Appendices

Appendix 1 Information and advice	193
Appendix 2 Useful addresses	195
Appendix 3 Abbreviations used in the notes	197

Index	199

Abbreviations

CA	carer's allowance
CTC	child tax credit
DLA	disability living allowance
DWP	Department for Work and Pensions
ESA	employment and support allowance
FE	further education
HB	housing benefit
HE	higher education
HMRC	HM Revenue and Customs
HNC	Higher National Certificate
HND	Higher National Diploma
IB	incapacity benefit
IS	income support
JSA	jobseeker's allowance
MA	maternity allowance
NI	national insurance
NQ	National Qualifications
PC	pension credit
PIP	personal independence payment
SAAS	Student Awards Agency Scotland
SAP	statutory adoption pay
SMP	statutory maternity pay
SPP	statutory paternity pay
SSS	Social Security Scotland
SSP	statutory sick pay
SSPP	statutory shared parental pay
SVQ	Scottish Vocational Qualification
UC	universal credit
WTC	working tax credit

Means-tested benefit rates 2019/20

Universal credit

Standard allowance £pm
Single	Under 25	251.77
	25 or over	317.82
Couple	Both under 25	395.20
	One or both 25 or over	498.89

Elements
Eldest child		277.08
Second and each subsequent child who qualifies		231.67
Disabled child	Lower rate	126.11
	Higher rate	392.08
Limited capability for work (some claims only)		126.11
Limited capability for work-related activity		336.20
Carer		160.20

Childcare costs
One child	up to £646.35
Two or more children	up to £1,108.04
Percentage of childcare costs covered	85%

Income support and income-based jobseeker's allowance

Personal allowance		£pw
Single	Under 25	57.90
	25 or over	73.10
Lone parent	Under 18	57.90
	18 or over	73.10
Couple	Both under 18 (maximum)	87.50
	One 18 or over (maximum)	114.85
	Both 18 or over	114.85

Premiums		
Carer		36.85
Disability	Single	34.35
	Couple	48.95
Enhanced disability	Single	16.80
	Couple	24.10
Severe disability	One qualifies	65.85
	Two qualify	131.70
Pensioner (couple)		140.40

Income-related employment and support allowance

Personal allowance	Assessment phase £pw	Main phase £pw
Single		
Under 25	57.90	73.10
25 or over	73.10	73.10
Lone parent		
Under 18	57.90	73.10
18 or over	73.10	73.10
Couple		
Both under 18 (maximum)	87.50	114.85
Both 18 or over	114.85	114.85
Premiums		
Carer	36.85	36.85
Severe disability		
One qualifies	65.85	65.85
Two qualify	131.70	131.70
Enhanced disability		
Single	16.80	16.80
Couple	24.10	24.10
Pensioner		
Couple, usual rate	140.40	111.35
Couple, support group		101.85
Components		
Work-related activity (some claims only)		29.05
Support		38.55

Housing benefit
Personal allowance

Single	Under 25	57.90
	Under 25 (on main phase employment and support allowance)	73.10
	25 or over	73.10
Lone parent	Under 18	57.90
	Under 18 (on main phase employment and support allowance)	73.10
	18 or over	73.10
Couple	Both under 18	87.50
	Both under 18 (claimant on main phase employment and support allowance)	114.85
	One or both 18 or over	114.85
Children (under 20)		66.90

Over pension age (and not on income support, income-based jobseeker's allowance, income-related employment and support allowance or universal credit)

	Single	181.00
	Couple	270.60

Premiums

Family (only pre-1 May 2016 claims with a child already in the family)

	Standard rate	17.45
	Some lone parents	22.20
Carer		36.85
Disability	Single	34.35
	Couple	48.95
Disabled child		64.19
Severe disability	One qualifies	65.85
	Two qualify	131.70
Enhanced disability	Single	16.80
	Couple	24.10
	Child	26.04

Components

Work-related activity (some claims only)	29.05
Support	38.55

Non-means-tested benefit rates 2019/20

	£pw
Attendance allowance	
Higher rate	87.65
Lower rate	58.70
Bereavement benefits	
Bereavement support payment (maximum lump sum)	3,500
Bereavement support payment (maximum monthly rate)	350
Carer's allowance	66.15
Child benefit	
Only/eldest child	20.70
Other child(ren)	13.70
Disability living allowance	
Care component	
Highest	87.65
Middle	58.70
Lowest	23.20
Mobility component	
Higher	61.20
Lower	23.20
Employment and support allowance (contributory)	
Assessment phase	
Basic allowance (under 25)	57.90
Basic allowance (25 or over)	73.10
Main phase	
Basic allowance (16 or over)	73.10
Work-related activity component (some claims only)	29.05
Support component	38.55
Guardian's allowance	17.60

Jobseeker's allowance (contribution-based)
Under 25 — 57.90
25 or over — 73.10

Maternity allowance
Standard rate — 148.68
Variable rate — 90% of earnings

Personal independence payment
Daily living component
Enhanced rate — 87.65
Standard rate — 58.70

Mobility component
Enhanced rate — 61.20
Standard rate — 23.20

Retirement pensions
State pension — 168.60
Category A — 129.20

Statutory adoption pay — 145.18

Statutory maternity pay
Standard rate — 145.18
Variable rate — 90% of earnings

Statutory paternity pay — 148.68

Statutory shared parental pay — 148.68

Statutory sick pay — 94.25

Tax credit rates 2019/20

Child tax credit	£ per day	£ per year
Family element (some claims only)	1.49	545
Child element	7.60	2,780
Disabled child element	9.17	3,355
Severely disabled child element	3.72	1,360

Working tax credit		
Basic element	5.36	1,960
Couple element	5.50	2,010
Lone parent element	5.50	2,010
30-hour element	2.22	810
Disabled worker element	8.65	3,165
Severe disability element	3.73	1,365
Childcare element		
Eligible childcare costs to a weekly maximum of:		
One child		70% of £175
Two or more children		70% of £300

Income thresholds		
Working tax credit only or with child tax credit		6,420
Child tax credit only		16,105

How to use this *Handbook*

This *Handbook* is intended for students and those who advise students, or potential students, in Scotland about their entitlement to benefits and tax credits. It outlines the benefit and tax credit rules and focuses on issues relevant to students. It covers both further and higher education. For more detailed information on the rules, see CPAG's *Welfare Benefits and Tax Credits Handbook*.

This *Handbook* covers rules affecting students studying in Scotland who are eligible for support through Scottish funding bodies such as the Student Awards Agency Scotland. It does not cover the rules for students getting support from England, Wales or Northern Ireland, or elsewhere outside Scotland.

Up to date

This *Handbook* was up to date on 1 July 2019 and is intended to be used for the academic year 2019/20. Rates of grants and loans used are those for the 2019/20 academic year. Benefit and tax credit rates used are those from April 2019.

Check CPAG's online version of this *Handbook* for updates in April 2020 at www.onlinepublications.cpag.org.uk.

Full-time students

Most full-time students are excluded from benefits, mainly those benefits where entitlement relies on a means test. There is one definition of 'full-time student' used for most means-tested benefits – ie, income support, jobseeker's allowance, employment and support allowance and housing benefit. Other definitions are used for universal credit (UC), carer's allowance and for council tax. Some students, however, can claim means-tested benefits despite being classed as full time. If you are excluded from one benefit, do not therefore assume that you are excluded from all of them. Who counts as a 'full-time student', or as 'receiving education' for UC, is explained in detail in the relevant chapters.

Structure of the *Handbook*

A benefit chart on pxx provides an overview of benefit and tax credit entitlement for students. You may want to use this as a starting point to check possible entitlement and then use the individual chapters for details.

Part 1 looks at students' entitlement to benefits and tax credits. **Part 2** gives a glossary of student support in further and higher education, and **Part 3** considers how each kind of support affects entitlement to universal credit, other means-tested benefits, tax credits and health benefits. **Part 4** considers other matters – council tax and benefits if you take time out from your studies.

Chapters have endnotes with references to the legal sources. Where an abbreviation is used in the endnotes or in the text, this is explained in Appendix 3 and on px. If you are appealing against a benefit or tax credit decision, you may want to refer to the law. Appendix 1 suggests where you can find legislation and caselaw.

Further information, training and advice

CPAG, with Scottish government funding, continues to make this *Handbook* available free online at www.onlinepublications.cpag.org.uk, and provides training, advice and information to advisers in Scotland on benefits for people who are studying or thinking of studying. Please contact Angela Toal on 0141 552 8361, or see https://cpag.org.uk/scotland/welfare-rights/students-benefits for details of the support we offer. If you are an adviser and have a specific query on benefits and students, contact our advice line on 0141 552 0552 between 10am and 4pm Monday to Thursday or between 10am and 12 noon on Fridays, or email advice@cpagscotland.org.uk.

Please send any comments, corrections or suggestions for inclusion in the next edition to CPAG in Scotland, Unit 9, Ladywell, 94 Duke Street, Glasgow G4 0UW; email: staff@cpagscotland.org.uk.

Benefits and tax credits: overview

The following chart summarises the benefits and tax credits you may be able to claim depending on your circumstances. In each case, there are other tests you must pass to be entitled. The page number in the last column takes you to the relevant chapter, where you will find more details about the rules of entitlement. Part 3 explains which benefits are affected by any grant or loan you get. Terms such as 'full time', 'part time' and 'student' are explained in each benefit chapter. **Note:** new claims cannot usually be made for income support, income-based jobseeker's allowance, income-related employment and support allowance, housing benefit and tax credits.

Your circumstances	Benefit or tax credit	Page
Aged 16–18 (and some 19-year-olds) in full-time further education		
Have a child	Income support	p51
	Housing benefit	p37
	Child tax credit	p101
	Child benefit	p8
	Universal credit	p89
Aged 16–20 (and some 21-year-olds) in full-time further education		
Orphan, estranged or separated from parents	Income support	p51
	Housing benefit	p37
	Universal credit	p89
Living away from parents	Housing benefit	p37
Full-time student		
Single	Health benefits	p31
Lone parent of child under five	Income support	p51
	Housing benefit	p37
	Child tax credit	p101
	Child benefit	p8
	Universal credit	p89

Your circumstances	Benefit or tax credit	Page
Student couple with a child, or lone parent		
Long vacation	Jobseeker's allowance	p68
	Income support (if eligible)	p51
All year	Housing benefit	p37
	Child tax credit	p101
	Child benefit	p8
	Universal credit	p89
Couple, one student	Income support	p51
	Jobseeker's allowance	p68
	Employment and support allowance	p20
	Housing benefit	p37
	Child tax credit	p101
	Child benefit	p8
	Universal credit	p89
Part-time student	Income support	p51
	Jobseeker's allowance	p68
	Employment and support allowance	p20
	Housing benefit	p37
	Universal credit	p89
Working		
Under 16 hours		
Part-time student	Income support	p51
	Jobseeker's allowance	p68
Full-time student	Income support (if eligible)	p51
At least 16 hours a week (24 for most couples) and have a child	Working tax credit	p108
At least 16 hours a week and have a disability	Working tax credit	p108
At least 30 hours a week and aged 25 or over	Working tax credit	p108
At least 16 hours a week and aged 60 or over	Working tax credit	p108
Any number of hours	Universal credit (if eligible)	p89

Your circumstances	Benefit or tax credit	Page
Sick or disabled	Employment and support allowance	p20
	Housing benefit	p37
	Personal independence payment	p85
	Health benefits	p31
	Universal credit	p89
Recovered and waiting to return to studies	Housing benefit	p37
	Jobseeker's allowance	p68
	Universal credit	p89
Having a baby		
Under 18	Best Start foods	p115
	Best Start grant	p114
Getting certain benefits/tax credits	Best Start foods	p115
	Best Start grant	p114
Working or recently working	Maternity allowance	p81
	Statutory maternity pay	p80
	Statutory shared parental pay	p81
	Working tax credit	p108
	Universal credit	p89
When the child is born	Child tax credit	p101
	Child benefit	p8
	Universal credit	p89
Studying part time	Income support	p51
Partner having a baby	Statutory paternity pay	p81
	Statutory shared parental pay	p81
Adopting a child	Statutory adoption pay	p81
Caring for someone sick or disabled		
Studying part time	Carer's allowance	p3
	Income support	p51
	Universal credit	p89
Waiting to return to studies after taking time out to care	Jobseeker's allowance	p68
	Housing benefit	p37
	Universal credit	p89
Need dental treatment or glasses	Health benefits	p31
Reached pension age	Pension credit	
	Housing benefit	p37

Part 1
Benefits and tax credits

Chapter 1
Carer's allowance

This chapter covers:
1. What is carer's allowance (below)
2. Who is eligible (p4)
3. Amount of benefit (p5)
4. Claiming carer's allowance (p5)
5. Challenging a decision (p5)
6. Other benefits and tax credits (p6)

Basic facts
– Carer's allowance (CA) is paid to people who care for someone with a severe disability.
– Part-time students are eligible to claim.
– Full-time students cannot claim.
– CA is not means tested, but you cannot get it if you work and earn more than £123 a week.
– Getting CA qualifies you for a carer element in universal credit or a carer premium in your income support, income-based jobseeker's allowance, income-related employment and support allowance and housing benefit.

1. What is carer's allowance

Carer's allowance (CA) is for people who spend at least 35 hours a week looking after a disabled person (an adult or child). The disabled person must be getting attendance allowance, the middle or highest rate of disability living allowance care component, the daily living component of personal independence payment, armed forces independence payment or constant attendance allowance in respect of an industrial or war disablement. The amount of CA you get is not means tested and your student loan, grant or other income does not affect it. Part-time students can get CA, but full-time students are not eligible.

Note: the Scottish government pays a supplement to people living in Scotland who get CA, which increases the amount of their CA to the level of jobseeker's allowance. It is paid as a lump sum every six months. A one-off £300 young carer grant for 16–18-year-old carers who cannot get CA is due to be introduced in Scotland in autumn 2019 (see p7). At the time of writing, the regulations were not finalised, but it is expected that eligible young carers will be those providing care for at least 16 hours a week in total, for up to three people who get certain benefits. See https://cpag.org.uk/scotland/welfare-rights/scottish-benefits for more information on these payments.

2. Who is eligible

You are eligible if you are a part-time student and you satisfy the basic rules on p5. You are not eligible if you are in full-time education.

Full-time education

You are in full-time education if an overall consideration of your course requirements and your performance against these suggests this. If you are on a full-time course of education, you are normally taken to be in full-time education for the purpose of carer's allowance (CA).[1] If you think that, given your circumstances, you are not in full-time education, you may be able to argue that you are a part-time student.[2]

You are also treated as being in full-time education if you 'attend a course' (see below) at a university, college or other educational establishment for 21 hours or more a week.[3] These 21 hours include not just classes, lectures and seminars, but also individual study for course work. Meal breaks and unsupervised study are ignored. However, you are regarded as studying under supervision if you are doing course work, whether at home or at college, alone or in the presence of a supervisor.[4] Unsupervised study is work beyond the requirements of the course.

If your college or university says that it expects students to spend 21 hours or more a week in supervised study and classes, the DWP usually assumes that you are in full-time education.

In practice, if you want to show that you spend fewer hours on course work than the college or university expects, you need to provide detailed evidence and be prepared to appeal. If your particular circumstances mean that you are not expected to satisfy the normal requirements of the course (eg, because you are exempt from certain subjects), you may be able to argue that your hours of study are fewer than those expected of other students on the course.[5]

Time out from a course

'**Attending**' a course means being enrolled on and pursuing a course.[6] You are treated as still being in full-time education during short and long vacations, and until the course ends or you abandon it or are dismissed from it. You are still regarded as being in full-time education during temporary interruptions.[7] If you

Chapter 1: Carer's allowance
5. Challenging a decision

have taken time out to care for someone and the interruption is not temporary (eg, if you have agreed with your institution to take a whole year out of your course), you may be able to claim CA.[8]

Basic rules

As well as being a student who is eligible to claim, to qualify for CA you must satisfy all of the following conditions.[9]
- You are aged 16 or over.
- You spend at least 35 hours a week caring for someone.
- The person for whom you care gets the middle or highest rate of disability living allowance care component, the daily living component of personal independence payment, attendance allowance, constant attendance allowance or armed forces independence payment.
- You are not working and earning more than £123 a week.
- You satisfy certain rules on residence and presence in the UK and are not a 'person subject to immigration control'. See CPAG's *Welfare Benefits and Tax Credits Handbook* for details.

3. Amount of benefit

The amount of carer's allowance (CA) is £66.15 a week (April 2019 rate). In Scotland, you are also paid a supplement to increase your CA to the level of jobseeker's allowance. This is paid in two lump-sum payments each year.

4. Claiming carer's allowance

You claim carer's allowance on Form DS700, available from local Jobcentre Plus offices or from www.gov.uk/government/publications/carers-allowance-claim-form. You can also claim online at www.gov.uk/carers-allowance/how-to-claim. Your claim can be backdated for up to three months if you qualified during that earlier period.

Benefit is usually paid directly into a bank account.

5. Challenging a decision

If you think a decision about your carer's allowance is wrong, you can ask the DWP to look at it again. This process is known as a 'mandatory reconsideration'. Provided you ask within the time limit (usually one month), the DWP notifies you of the decision in a 'mandatory reconsideration notice'. If you are still not

Chapter 1: Carer's allowance
6. Other benefits and tax credits

happy when you get this notice, you can appeal to the independent First-tier Tribunal. If it was not possible to ask the DWP to reconsider the decision within a month, you can ask for a late revision (within 13 months), explaining why it is late. You can also ask the DWP to look at a decision again at any time if certain grounds are met – eg, if there has been an official error.

6. Other benefits and tax credits

The benefit cap does not apply if you get carer's allowance (CA).

The disabled person's benefit

Your entitlement to CA depends on the person for whom you care continuing to get her/his disability benefit. If her/his benefit stops, your benefit should also stop. To avoid being overpaid, make sure you tell the Carer's Allowance Unit if the disabled person's attendance allowance, disability living allowance, personal independence payment or armed forces independence payment stops being paid.

Note: although CA may mean more money for you, it may result in the person for whom you care losing some income support (IS), income-related employment and support allowance (ESA), pension credit or housing benefit (HB). If s/he lives alone, s/he may be getting a severe disability premium included in the assessment of these benefits. S/he cannot continue to get this premium if you get CA for her/him. See CPAG's *Welfare Benefits and Tax Credits Handbook* for details and, if in doubt, get advice before claiming.

Overlapping benefits

Although CA is not means tested, you cannot receive it at the same time as incapacity benefit, maternity allowance, severe disablement allowance, widowed parent's allowance, retirement pension, contribution-based jobseeker's allowance (JSA) or contributory ESA. If you are eligible for more than one benefit, you get whichever is worth the most.

Getting a carer premium or element

If you are a part-time student getting CA and claiming universal credit (UC), you are eligible for a carer element in your UC and you are not expected to look for work. If you are getting IS, income-based JSA, income-related ESA or HB, an extra carer premium is included in these benefits, even if your CA is not being paid because you are getting another benefit that overlaps with it.

Working tax credit

If you have a child(ren) and a partner and you get CA, you are eligible for working tax credit if your partner works at least 16 hours a week, rather than the usual 24.

Chapter 1: Carer's allowance
Notes

Carer's allowance supplement

If you get carer's allowance on a 'qualifying date', you are entitled to a top-up payment from Social Security Scotland called a 'carer's allowance supplement'. Each payment covers a six-month period. The qualifying dates for 2019 are 15 April and 14 October, and the amount payable each time is £226.20. You must actually be receiving CA on the qualifying date – an 'underlying entitlement' is not enough. The CA supplement is disregarded for all means-tested benefits and tax credits. There is no need to make a claim for CA supplement – it should be paid automatically.

Young carer grant

A young carer grant paid by Social Security Scotland is to be introduced in autumn 2019. The following information is provisional, as the regulations were not finalised at the time of writing. The young carer grant is a one-off grant of £300, payable once a year. Eligible young carers are those aged 16–18 (regardless of their circumstances) who are not getting CA. To qualify, you must be providing care for at least 16 hours a week in total, although this can be a combination of care for up to three people. The cared-for person(s) must be in receipt of one of the benefits that allows entitlement to CA (see p3).

For up-to-date information on the young carer grant, see www.cpag.org.uk/scottish-benefits/carers-assistance.

Notes

2. **Who is eligible**
   1 *SSWP v Deane* [2010] EWCA Civ 699
   2 CG/1154/2010
   3 Reg 5 SS(ICA) Regs
   4 *Flemming v SSWP* [2002] EWCA Civ 641; *Wright-Turner v Department for Social Development* [2002] NICA 2
   5 CG/3189/2004
   6 *Flemming v SSWP* [2002] EWCA Civ 641
   7 Reg 5(3) SS(ICA) Regs
   8 *SM v SSWP* [2016] UKUT 406 (AAC); Memo DMG 2/17
   9 s70 SSCBA 1992

Chapter 2
Child benefit

This chapter covers:
1. What is child benefit (below)
2. Who is eligible (below)
3. Amount of benefit (p12)
4. Claiming child benefit (p12)
5. Challenging a decision (p12)
6. Other benefits and tax credits (p13)

Basic facts
– Child benefit is paid to people who are responsible for a child or a 'qualifying young person'.
– Both full-time and part-time students can claim child benefit.
– If you are under 20, someone else may be able to claim child benefit for you if you are studying.
– Child benefit is not means tested.

1. What is child benefit

Child benefit is paid to people who are responsible for a child or 'qualifying young person'. You do not have to have paid national insurance contributions to qualify for child benefit. It is not means tested, so the amount you get is not affected by your student loan, grant or other income. If you earn over £50,000 and you or your partner get child benefit, you may have extra income tax to pay (known as the 'high-income child benefit charge').

2. Who is eligible

You qualify for child benefit if:[1]
- you are responsible for a child or 'qualifying young person' – ie:
  – s/he lives with you; or

– you contribute to the cost of supporting her/him at a rate of at least the amount of child benefit for her/him; *and*
- you have priority over other potential claimants. Only one person can get child benefit for a particular child. There is an order of priority for who receives it where two or more people would otherwise be entitled; *and*
- you are 'present and ordinarily resident' in Britain, not a 'person subject to immigration control' and have a 'right to reside'. These terms are explained in CPAG's *Welfare Benefits and Tax Credits Handbook*.

You do not have to be the child's parent to claim child benefit for her/him.

Being a student, whether full or part time, does not affect your entitlement to child benefit.

If you are a 'qualifying young person' (see below), your parent or someone else who is responsible for you may be able to claim child benefit. You cannot, however, claim child benefit for yourself.

If a qualifying young person gets universal credit, income support, income-based jobseeker's allowance, employment and support allowance, working tax credit or child tax credit in her/his own right, any child benefit paid for the young person stops.

If a young person lives with a partner, or is married or in a civil partnership, you can get child benefit for her/him if s/he lives with you or you still contribute to her/his support, but only if her/his partner is in 'relevant education' (see p52) or approved training. The young person's partner cannot be the claimant.

In some circumstances, special rules apply – eg, if your child is being looked after by a local authority or is in prison or a young offenders' institution.

Who counts as a child

Anyone aged under 16 counts as a '**child**' for child benefit purposes, whether or not s/he goes to school. Provided you meet the other qualifying conditions, child benefit can be paid for her/him.[2] Child benefit can also be paid for a child after s/he reaches 16 until at least 31 August after her/his 16th birthday, and then for as long as s/he continues to count as a 'qualifying young person'.

Who counts as a qualifying young person

A '**qualifying young person**' is someone who:[3]
- is aged 16 and has left full-time non-advanced education (see p10) or training. This only applies up to 31 August after her/his 16th birthday (but see p10); *or*
- is aged 16 or 17, has left education or training and satisfies the extension period rule (see p10); *or*
- is aged 16 or over but under 20 and is on a course of full-time non-advanced education (see p10) not provided as a result of her/his employment, or

Chapter 2: Child benefit
2. Who is eligible

approved training not provided under a contract of employment. 'Approved training' is defined as Employability Fund activity.[4] The young person must have started the course or training before reaching 19, or have been accepted or enrolled to undertake it before that age; *or*
- is aged 16 or over but under 20 and has finished a course of full-time non-advanced education not provided as a result of her/his employment, or approved training not provided under a contract of employment, but is accepted or enrolled on another such course. **Note:** if the course s/he has finished is an approved training course, this only applies if the following course is also approved training. Although someone must have started, or been accepted or enrolled on, the training or education when s/he was under 19 to be a qualifying young person once the course begins, the rules do not specify this for the gap between courses.[5] If the young person was accepted or enrolled after reaching age 19, you can argue that s/he is a qualifying young person from the end of the course until the next course begins; *or*
- is aged 16 or over but under 20 and has left full-time non-advanced education (see below) or approved training but has not passed her/his terminal date (see p11).

Full-time non-advanced education
'**Full time**' is more than 12 hours a week of classes and supervised study during term time.
'**Non-advanced education**' is anything below degree, Higher National Certificate or Higher National Diploma level, and includes school-level courses, Scottish Vocational Qualification levels 1–3, National Certificates, National Progression Awards and Scottish Wider Access Programme courses.

If your child counts as a qualifying young person on more than one of the above grounds, s/he counts as a qualifying young person until the last day that applies.[6]

If you stop being entitled to child benefit for your child because s/he no longer counts as a qualifying young person, but s/he later satisfies one of the above conditions again and so counts as a qualifying young person once more, child benefit can again become payable for her/him. **Note:** in some cases, you can continue to claim during such an interruption – eg, if the young person is ill or the gap is less than six months. In both cases, the interruption must be accepted as being reasonable.[7]

Note: in the rest of this chapter, the term 'child' is used to mean both children under 16 and qualifying young people aged 16 or over.

The extension period

If your child is 16 or 17, s/he continues to count as a qualifying young person, and so child benefit can continue to be paid for her/him, during an 'extension period' if:[8]

- s/he has left education or training; *and*
- s/he is registered as available for work, education or training with Skills Development Scotland; *and*
- s/he is not in remunerative work – ie, work of 24 hours a week or more for payment or in expectation of payment; *and*
- you were entitled to child benefit for her/him immediately before the extension period started; *and*
- you apply in writing or by phone within three months of the date your child's education or training finished.

In this context, 'education' and 'training' are not defined and so may mean any kind of education or training.

The extension period starts from the Monday after your child's course of education or training ends and lasts for 20 weeks from that date. If your child reaches 18 during the extension period, unless s/he counts as a qualifying young person on another ground (see p9), your child benefit for her/him ends from the first child benefit payday on or after which s/he reaches 18.[9]

The terminal date

If your child leaves full-time non-advanced education (see p52) or approved training before reaching 20, s/he continues to count as a qualifying young person until either:[10]

- the 'terminal date' (see below); *or*
- her/his 20th birthday, if this falls before the terminal date.

The general rule means that unless s/he continues to count as a qualifying young person on another ground or is returning to sit an exam (see below), you stop receiving child benefit for her/him on that date.

> **The terminal date**
> Your child's **'terminal date'** is the first of the following dates that falls after the date her/his full-time non-advanced education or approved training finishes:
> – the last day in February;
> – the last day in May;
> – the last day in August;
> – the last day in November.

If someone is doing a Higher Certificate or Advanced Higher Certificate and leaves full-time non-advanced education earlier than s/he would have done if s/he were doing a comparable course in England and Wales, the terminal date is the one that would have applied had s/he had been doing the comparable course.[11]

A child who returns to sit an external examination in connection with her/his course of relevant education is treated as still being in relevant education until the date of the last exam.[12]

3. Amount of benefit

Weekly rate from April 2019
Eldest eligible child   £20.70
Other children (each)   £13.70

Note: child benefit rates are frozen until April 2020.[13]

4. Claiming child benefit

Child benefit is administered by HM Revenue and Customs (HMRC). You claim child benefit on Form CH2, which you can get at www.gov.uk or from the Child Benefit Office on 0300 200 3100, HMRC's website (www.gov.uk/government/organisations/hm-revenue-customs) or from Jobcentre Plus offices.

You should make a claim within three months of becoming eligible. This is because your claim can usually only be backdated for up to three months. You do not have to show any reasons why your claim was late.

Getting paid

Child benefit is usually paid directly into your bank (or similar) account. Which account it goes into is up to you. If you do not want your benefit to go into an account that is overdrawn, give HMRC details of an alternative account if you have access to, or can open, one.

5. Challenging a decision

If you think a decision about your child benefit is wrong, you can ask HM Revenue and Customs (HMRC) to look at it again. This process is known as a 'mandatory reconsideration'. Provided you ask within the time limit (usually one month), HMRC notifies you of the decision in a 'mandatory reconsideration notice'. If you are still not happy when you get this notice, you can appeal to the independent First-tier Tribunal. If it was not possible to ask HMRC to reconsider the decision within a month, you can ask for a late revision (within 13 months), explaining why it is late. You can also ask HMRC to look at a decision again at any time if certain grounds are met – eg, if there has been an official error.

6. Other benefits and tax credits

If you get child benefit, you count as being responsible for a child for income support (IS) and income-based jobseeker's allowance (JSA), and usually for housing benefit (HB). This can help you qualify for these benefits in some circumstances while you are a full-time student (see Chapters 6, 7 and 8).

Child benefit is ignored as income for IS and income-based JSA if you are getting child tax credit. However, if you have been getting IS or income-based JSA since before 6 April 2004 which includes amounts for your child(ren), child benefit is taken into account as income. Child benefit is ignored as income for universal credit, income-related employment and support allowance and HB.

Child benefit is taken into account when calculating whether the benefit cap applies (see p49 and p98).

Notes

2. **Who is eligible**
 1 ss141-47 SSCBA 1992
 2 s142(1) SSCBA 1992; reg 4 CB Regs
 3 s142(2) SSCBA 1992; regs 2-8 CB Regs
 4 Reg 1(3) CB Regs
 5 Reg 3 CB Regs
 6 Reg 2(2) CB Regs
 7 Reg 6 CB Regs
 8 Reg 5 CB Regs
 9 Reg 14 The Child Benefit and Guardian's Allowance (Administration) Regulations 2003, No.492; reg 5(3) CB Regs
 10 Reg 7 CB Regs
 11 Reg 7(2) case 1.3 CB Regs
 12 Reg 7(2) case 2.1 CB Regs

3. **Amount of benefit**
 13 s11(2) WRWA 2016

Chapter 3
Disability living allowance

This chapter covers:
1. What is disability living allowance (below)
2. Who is eligible (p15)
3. Amount of benefit (p18)
4. Claiming disability living allowance (p18)
5. Challenging a decision (p18)
6. Other benefits and tax credits (p19)

Basic facts
- Disability living allowance (DLA) is paid to disabled people who need personal care or who have mobility difficulties.
- You must be under 16 to make a new claim.
- Getting DLA allows you to claim universal credit as a full-time student, provided you satisfy certain other conditions.
- Getting DLA allows you to claim income-related employment and support allowance as a full-time student. You may also be able to claim housing benefit as a full-time student and you may get a disability premium.
- DLA is not means tested.

1. What is disability living allowance

Disability living allowance (DLA) is a benefit for disabled people who need help with personal care or who have mobility difficulties. Unless you are under 16, you cannot make a new claim for DLA and must claim personal independence payment (PIP) instead (see p85).

DLA has two components:
- care component, paid at either the lowest, middle or highest rate;
- mobility component, paid at either the lower or higher rate.

You can get either or both components.

Students already getting DLA can continue to do so, but will be invited to claim PIP instead at some point. Starting college or university does not usually lead the DWP to reassess your entitlement to DLA.

The amount you get is not means tested, and so is not reduced because of student support or other income.

If you are a full-time student getting DLA and you satisfy certain other conditions, you are eligible for universal credit (see p90). If you are a full-time student and get DLA, you are eligible for income-related employment and support allowance. You may also be eligible for housing benefit.

Note: from summer 2020, DLA for children will be replaced in Scotland by 'disability assistance for children and young people'.

2. Who is eligible

Full-time and part-time students can continue to get disability living allowance (DLA). You cannot make a new claim unless you are under 16, but should claim personal independence payment (PIP) instead if you think you may be entitled.

If you get DLA and your condition changes which means you should qualify for a different rate of DLA (see below), or your DLA award is due to end, or you turn 16, you must claim PIP instead. Otherwise, at some point you will be reassessed for PIP.

Care component

To get the care component, you must have a physical or mental disability that means you need the following kinds of care from another person. What is important is the help you need rather than the help you actually get.

You get paid either the lowest, middle or highest rate.

Lowest rate

You get the lowest rate if you meet either (or both) of these two conditions.
- You need attention in connection with your bodily functions (see p16) for a significant portion of the day. This attention might be given all at once or be spread out. It should normally add up to about an hour or more, or be made up of several brief periods.
- You cannot prepare a cooked meal for yourself if you have the ingredients. This is a test of whether you can manage all the tasks involved in preparing a main meal for one on a traditional cooker – eg, planning the meal, reading labels, chopping vegetables, carrying pans and using the cooker.

Middle rate

This is for people who need care either during the day or during the night, but not both. You get the middle rate if you meet one (or both) of the day care conditions *or* one (or both) of the night care conditions.

Care during the day
- You need frequent attention throughout the day in connection with your bodily functions (see below). This means you may qualify if you need help several times, not just once or twice, spread out throughout the day. If you need help just in the mornings and evenings, for instance, you might get the lowest rate instead.
- You need continual supervision throughout the day in order to avoid substantial danger to yourself or others. The supervision must be frequent or regular, but need not be continuous.

Care at night
- You need prolonged or repeated attention at night in connection with your bodily functions (see below). You should qualify if you need help once in the night for 20 minutes or more. You should also qualify if you need help twice in the night (or more often), however long it takes.
- In order to avoid substantial danger to yourself or others, you need another person to be awake at night for a prolonged period (20 minutes) or at frequent intervals (three times or more) to watch over you.

Highest rate

This is for people who need care during both the day and night. You get the highest rate if you meet one (or both) of the above day care conditions and one (or both) of the above night care conditions. You also get the highest rate if you are terminally ill – ie, you have a progressive disease and could reasonably be expected to die within six months.

Attention with bodily functions

This is help from someone else to do personal things you cannot do entirely by yourself. 'Bodily functions' are things like breathing, hearing, seeing, eating, drinking, walking, sitting, sleeping, getting in or out of bed, dressing, undressing, and using the toilet. However, any help in connection with an impaired bodily function can count if it involves personal contact (physical or verbal in your presence) and it is reasonably required.

For example, a blind student might need the help of a notetaker or reader, or a guide around campus or around town. A deaf student might need an interpreter. A student with arthritis might need help getting in and out of chairs.

You must need the help of another person to qualify for DLA. If you only need artificial aids, you cannot get DLA.

You cannot count help with domestic chores, unless someone is helping you to do them for yourself.

If you have dyslexia, you could argue that you qualify for DLA, but only if you need someone to be with you to help you read and write – ie, someone sitting beside you reading to you or helping you develop reading skills.[1] This could count as attention with the bodily function of seeing or of the brain.[2]

Having a social life

The kind of help you need must be reasonably required. This means that you need it to enable you as far as reasonably possible to live a normal life. You can include help needed to take part in social activities, sport, recreation, cultural or political activities, provided the help required is in connection with a bodily function.

Mobility component

There are two rates of the mobility component.

Lower rate

This is for people who can walk, but need guidance or supervision. You qualify if you are able to walk but, because of your disability, you cannot walk outdoors without guidance or supervision from someone else most of the time.

You can still qualify if you are able to manage on familiar routes. If you cannot manage without guidance or supervision on unfamiliar routes or you cannot manage anywhere, you should qualify. For example, someone with learning disabilities may qualify even if s/he has learned the route to and from home and college if s/he still needs guidance in other places.

Higher rate

This is for people who cannot walk or have great difficulty walking because of a physical disability. You qualify if:
- you are unable to walk; *or*
- you have no legs or feet; *or*
- you are virtually unable to walk. This takes account of the distance you can walk before you experience severe discomfort. There is no set distance at which you pass or fail this test. Some people have passed who can walk 100 metres; others have failed who can walk only 50 metres. The speed at which you walk and how you walk also count; *or*
- the exertion required to walk would be dangerous or could cause a serious deterioration in your health; *or*
- you are deaf and blind; *or*
- you have a severe visual impairment.

Someone who is severely mentally impaired may also qualify if s/he gets the highest rate care component and meets other conditions.

Chapter 3: Disability living allowance
5. Challenging a decision

Claiming for children

You can claim DLA for a disabled child. There is no lower age limit for the care component, but the cooked meal condition for the lowest rate does not apply to children under age 16. You can claim the higher rate mobility component for your child from age three and the lower rate mobility component from age five.

Because all children need care or supervision to some extent, there is an extra test. As well as passing the disability test, children under 16 must have needs substantially in excess of the normal requirements of other children their age to qualify for the care component. For the lower rate mobility component, children under 16 must need substantially more guidance or supervision than other children of their age.

3. Amount of benefit

Weekly rate from April 2019

Care component
Lowest rate	£23.20
Middle rate	£58.70
Highest rate	£87.65

Mobility component
Lower rate	£23.20
Higher rate	£61.20

4. Claiming disability living allowance

You cannot make a new claim for disability living allowance (DLA) unless you are under 16; you must claim personal independence payment (PIP) instead (see p85).

If you still get DLA, you will be reassessed for PIP at some point.

DLA is usually paid directly into your bank account, and usually paid every four weeks in arrears.

5. Challenging a decision

If you think a decision about your disability living allowance is wrong, you can ask the DWP to look at it again. This process is known as a 'mandatory reconsideration'. Provided you ask within the time limit (usually one month), the

DWP notifies you of the decision in a 'mandatory reconsideration notice'. If you are still not happy when you get this notice, you can appeal to the independent First-tier Tribunal. If it was not possible to ask the DWP to reconsider the decision within a month, you can ask for a late revision (within 13 months), explaining why it is late. You can also ask the DWP to look at a decision again at any time if certain grounds are met – eg, if there has been an official error.

6. Other benefits and tax credits

If you meet certain other conditions and are a full-time student getting disability living allowance (DLA), you are eligible for universal credit (UC) (see p89). If you are a full-time student and get DLA, you are eligible for income-related employment and support allowance (ESA). You may also be eligible for housing benefit (HB).

DLA is paid in addition to UC, income support (IS), ESA and HB, and may qualify you for an additional premium in IS, ESA and HB.

If you claim other benefits or tax credits, make sure the job centre, Tax Credit Office or local authority office dealing with your claim knows you or your child get DLA.

If you, your partner or a child for whom you are responsible get DLA, you are exempt from the benefit cap (see p49 and p98).

Notes

2. Who is eligible
1 CDLA/1983/2006; CDLA/3204/2006
2 *KM v SSWP (DLA)* [2013] UKUT 159 (AAC), reported as [2014] AACR 2

Chapter 4

Employment and support allowance

This chapter covers:
1. What is employment and support allowance (below)
2. Who is eligible (p21)
3. Limited capability for work (p23)
4. Amount of benefit (p24)
5. Claiming employment and support allowance (p29)
6. Challenging a decision (p29)
7. Other benefits and tax credits (p29)

Basic facts
– Employment and support allowance (ESA) is for people who are assessed as having limited capability for work because of their health or disability.
– There is an income-related and a contributory ESA.
– Part-time students who have limited capability for work and full-time students who get disability living allowance or personal independence payment are eligible for income-related ESA.
– Part-time and full-time students can claim contributory ESA if they have paid sufficient national insurance contributions.

1. What is employment and support allowance

Employment and support allowance (ESA) is for people who have limited capability for work because of illness or disability.[1]

There is a contributory and an income-related ESA. **Contributory ESA** is for people who have paid national insurance contributions. **Income-related ESA** is means tested and is for people whose income and capital are low enough. It is possible to receive one or both types of ESA.

Note: you cannot usually make a new claim for income-related ESA as it is in the process of being replaced by universal credit. However, an exception applies

Chapter 4: Employment and support allowance
2. Who is eligible

if you get, or got in the past month (and continue to satisfy the rules for it), a severe disability premium in your income-related ESA, income support, income-based jobseeker's allowance or housing benefit.

2. Who is eligible

As new claims cannot usually be made for income-related employment and support allowance (ESA) (see p20 for exceptions), most students getting income-related ESA will be those who were already on this before starting the course, and who are eligible for income-related ESA as a student. If you cannot claim income-related ESA, you may be able to get universal credit instead (see Chapter 11).

To qualify for ESA, you must meet all the basic conditions.[2]
- You have limited capability for work (see p23).
- You are aged 16 or over and under pension age.
- You are in Great Britain (although some absences are allowed – see CPAG's *Welfare Benefits and Tax Credits Handbook* for more details).
- You satisfy the rules for contributory ESA (see below) or income-related ESA (see below).
- You are not working, although some 'permitted work' is allowed. See CPAG's *Welfare Benefits and Tax Credits Handbook* for more details.

Contributory employment and support allowance

Contributory ESA is not means tested. To qualify, you must meet the basic conditions above and have paid sufficient national insurance contributions.[3] See CPAG's *Welfare Benefits and Tax Credits Handbook* for details on this. There are no special rules for students. The same rules apply if you are taking time out from your course because of ill health (see p184).

Income-related employment and support allowance

Income-related ESA is means tested. You are eligible if you are a part-time student and have limited capability for work. If you are a full-time student, you are only eligible if you get disability living allowance (DLA) or personal independence payment (PIP). The same rules apply if you are taking time out from your course because of ill health (see p184).

To qualify for income-related ESA while studying, you must satisfy the basic conditions above and all the following conditions.[4]
- You are either a full-time student (see p22) who is entitled to DLA (either component, paid at any rate – see p14) or PIP (either component paid at any rate – see p85), or you are a part-time student.[5]
- Your income is less than the set amount the law says you need to live on (known as your 'applicable amount') – see p26.

- You have no more than £16,000 capital.
- Your partner (if you have one) is not working 24 hours or more a week.
- You are in Great Britain, satisfy the 'habitual residence' and the 'right to reside' tests, and are not a 'person subject to immigration control'. These terms are explained in CPAG's *Welfare Benefits and Tax Credits Handbook*. Further advice is available from UKCISA (see Appendix 2).

Full-time student

You are a full-time student if you are:[6]
- under 20 and a 'qualifying young person' (see below); *or*
- 19 or over and a full-time student, unless you are aged 19 and count as being a qualifying young person (see below); *or*
- under 19 in full-time advanced education (see p23).

Under 20 and a qualifying young person

You are a 'qualifying young person' if you are 19 or under and attending a full-time course of non-advanced education which you were accepted on, enrolled on or started when you were under 19. If you are accepted on, enrol on or start the course on or after your 19th birthday, you are not a qualifying young person (see below). 'Non-advanced education' is anything below degree, Higher National Certificate or Higher National Diploma level and includes school-level courses. Your course is classed as 'full time' for income-related ESA if it is for more than 12 hours a week during term time. These 12 hours include classes and supervised study, but not meal breaks or unsupervised study either at home or at college. You may count as a qualifying young person in a gap between courses or for a period after you have finished a course (see p9).

19 or over and a full-time student

You count as a full-time student if you are undertaking a full-time course of study at an educational establishment. There are two definitions of 'full time' that apply: the first covers mostly courses of advanced education; the second covers most courses of non-advanced education.
- Your course is full time if it is classed as full time by the institution. If the institution describes the course as full time, you need convincing evidence to persuade the DWP otherwise, bearing in mind that what matters is the course itself rather than the hours you attend. This definition covers all courses of advanced education and any courses of non-advanced education not funded in whole or in part by the Scottish government at a further education (FE) college.
- Your course is full time if it involves more than 16 hours a week classroom or workshop learning under the direct guidance of teaching staff, or 16 hours or less if your hours are made up of more than 21 hours a week of structured study hours. What matters is the number of hours specified in a document signed by

the college. This is often called a 'learning agreement', but your college may refer to it by some other name. This definition applies if you are at an FE college, not undertaking a higher education course, and your course is fully or partly funded by the Scottish government. Courses funded by the Scottish government include school qualifications like National Qualifications from Access level to Advanced Higher, Scottish Vocational Qualifications and National Certificates.

Under 19 in full-time advanced education
If you are under 19 and in full-time advanced education rather than in non-advanced education, the rules on when you count as full time are the same as for those aged 19 or over (see p22).

3. Limited capability for work

One of the basic rules of entitlement to employment and support allowance (ESA) is that you must be assessed as having 'limited capability for work'. This means that your mental or physical condition makes it unreasonable to require you to work. You are normally assessed at a medical, known as the 'work capability assessment'. This also assesses whether you have 'limited capability for work-related activity'. If you are assessed as having both limited capability for work and limited capability for work-related activity, you are in the 'support group' and your ESA includes an amount called a 'support component'.

If you are assessed as only having limited capability for work, you are in the 'work-related activity group'. You are expected to attend work-focused interviews and may be required to undertake work-related activity. If you do not do so, your benefit may be reduced. If your claim began before 3 April 2017, your ESA includes a 'work-related activity component'. If it began on or after this date, it does not.

If you are assessed as not having limited capability for work, you are not entitled to ESA. However, you can challenge this decision if you disagree with it (see p29).

Most full-time students who get disability living allowance (DLA) or personal independence payment (PIP) and who are claiming income-related ESA are treated as having limited capability for work and do not have to satisfy this part of the test.[7] However, you must still satisfy the test if:
- you are a qualifying young person under 20; *or*
- you are claiming contributory ESA.

All students, unless they are in the support group, must take part in work-focused interviews and may have to undertake work-related activity as a condition of getting full benefit.[8]

Chapter 4: Employment and support allowance
4. Amount of benefit

If you are required to undertake full-time study as part of your work-related activity, you can continue to get ESA, whether or not you get DLA or PIP.[9]

Starting to study may prompt the DWP to call you for a reassessment, although this should not happen routinely. At the next assessment, your ability to perform the set activities is considered in the context of what you can do in a typical day, including your college or university routines. For example, you may be asked questions about your ability to get around campus, your ability to get to and from lectures, how long you can sit comfortably to study, or your ability to hold a pen to take notes or write essays.

The questions you are asked depend on which of the set activities (such as standing and sitting, manual dexterity and understanding communication) are relevant to your condition.

See CPAG's *Welfare Benefits and Tax Credits Handbook* for advice on medical examinations and what to do if you do not pass the assessment.

Example
Rachel is 29 and getting contributory ESA that includes a support component. She starts a full-time course of study in August 2019. She continues to be eligible for contributory ESA, but is called for a medical reassessment. Her condition is still the same, she passes the assessment and her contributory ESA continues.

4. **Amount of benefit**

Employment and support allowance (ESA) is payable after seven 'waiting days'. You are paid a limited amount of ESA during an initial 'assessment phase'. In most cases, this lasts 13 weeks. After this, you are then paid more in the 'main phase' that follows.

ESA is worked out as follows.

In the assessment phase, you get a basic allowance of contributory ESA. The amount of income-related ESA you get depends on your needs (your applicable amount) and how much income you have.

In the main phase, if you are in the support group, you get a support component of £38.55 a week. If you are in the work-related activity group and you claimed before 3 April 2017, you get a work-related activity component of £29.05 a week. If you claimed on or after 3 April 2017, no work-related activity component can be added. For income-related ESA, the component is added to your applicable amount and your income is then subtracted from your applicable amount. For contributory ESA, it is added to the basic allowance.

Contributory employment and support allowance

Weekly rate from April 2019[10]

Assessment phase, basic allowance (under 25)	£57.90
Assessment phase, basic allowance (25 or over)	£73.10
Main phase, basic allowance (16–24)	£73.10
Main phase, basic allowance (25 or over)	£73.10
Main phase, support component	£38.55
Main phase, work-related activity component (claims before 3 April 2017 only)	£29.05

Contributory ESA is paid for up to a year if you are in the work-related activity group, or indefinitely if you are in the support group.

Income-related employment and support allowance

The amount of income-related ESA you get depends on your circumstances and the circumstances of your partner.[11] The amount also depends on your income and capital. Go through the following steps to work out the amount of ESA to which you are entitled.

Step one: capital
If your capital is over £16,000, you cannot get income-related ESA (see p21). Some kinds of capital are ignored. For details, see CPAG's *Welfare Benefits and Tax Credits Handbook*.

Step two: work out your applicable amount
This is an amount for basic weekly needs. It is made up of:[12]
- personal allowances (see p27);
- premiums (see p27);
- a support component or, for claims before 3 April 2017, a work-related activity component (see p28);
- housing costs (see p28).

Step three: work out your weekly income
Chapter 17 explains how your loan, grant or other income is taken into account for ESA and how to work out your weekly income.

Step four: deduct weekly income from applicable amount
If your income is *less* than your applicable amount, your ESA equals the difference between the two.

Chapter 4: Employment and support allowance
4. Amount of benefit

If your income is *the same as or more than* your applicable amount, you cannot get ESA. You can claim again if your income decreases – eg, during the long vacation.

Income-related ESA tops up contributory ESA if you are entitled to both and the income-related amount is higher.

Example
Doreen is 23 and has cerebral palsy. She gets the standard rate of the daily living component of personal independence payment (PIP) and housing benefit (HB) which includes a severe disability premium. In August 2019 she leaves her job and starts a full-time National Certificate course. She claims ESA – she can still claim ESA, and cannot claim universal credit (UC), because she gets a severe disability premium in her HB. She is eligible for both contributory and income-related ESA.

Assessment phase:
Step one   Doreen has no savings or capital.
Step two   Her applicable amount is:
                 Basic allowance for herself = £73.10
                 Severe disability premium = £65.85
Step three   Her weekly income is:
                 £73.10 contributory ESA (PIP is disregarded).
Step four   She gets income-related ESA of £65.85.

Main phase:
Doreen is assessed as having limited capability for work and work-related activity and as being in the support group.
Step two   Her applicable amount is:
                 Basic allowance for herself (£73.10) and support component (£38.55) and severe disability premium (£65.85) and enhanced disability premium (£16.80) = £194.30
Step three   Her weekly income is:
                 £111.65 contributory ESA (£73.10 + support component of £38.55) (PIP is disregarded).
Step four   She gets income-related ESA of £82.65.

Applicable amount

Your applicable amount is worked out by adding together your personal allowances, premiums, the component that applies to you in the main phase and any eligible housing costs. It is usually possible to find out what the new rates will be from the beginning of December. Check the DWP website at www.gov.uk/government/organisations/department-for-work-pensions for a press release on social security uprating. The rates on p27 are from April 2019.

Chapter 4: Employment and support allowance
4. Amount of benefit

Personal allowance

Your personal allowance is paid at either the single, lone parent or couple rate depending on your situation. The amount depends on your age and whether you are in the assessment phase or the main phase (see p24).

	Assessment phase £	Main phase £
Single		
Under 25	57.90	73.10
25 or over	73.10	73.10
Lone parent		
Under 18	57.90	73.10
18 or over	73.10	73.10
Couple		
Both under 18 (higher rate)	87.50	114.85
Both under 18 (not eligible for higher rate)	57.90	73.10
One under 18, one 18 or over (higher rate)	114.85	114.85
One under 18, one 18–24 (not eligible for higher rate)	57.90	73.10
One under 18, one 25 or over (not eligible for higher rate)	73.10	73.10
Both 18 or over	114.85	114.85

If you are both under 18, you get the higher rate if:
- one of you is responsible for a child; *or*
- you and your partner would both be eligible to claim income-related ESA if you were single; *or*
- your partner would qualify for income support (IS) if s/he were single; *or*
- your partner would qualify for income-based jobseeker's allowance (JSA) or severe hardship payments of JSA.

If one of you is under 18 and the other is 18 or over, you get the higher rate if the younger partner would:
- qualify for IS or income-related ESA if s/he were single; *or*
- qualify for income-based JSA or severe hardship payments of JSA.

Premiums

Qualifying for premiums depends on your circumstances. You can qualify for the following.
- **Pensioner premium.** You or your partner must have reached pension age (see p60). If you are in a couple and one of you is over pension age and one of you is under pension age, you get £140.40. In the main phase, these amounts are

reduced by the amount of the work-related activity component (if applicable) or support component for which you qualify.
- **Carer premium** of £36.85. The qualifying conditions are the same as for IS (see p63).
- **Enhanced disability premium.** You qualify for this if you or your partner get the highest rate of the disability living allowance (DLA) care component, the enhanced rate of the daily living component of PIP or if you get the support component of ESA. You get £16.80, or £24.10 if you are a couple.
- **Severe disability premium.** This is for severely disabled people who live alone, or who can be treated as living alone. You qualify if you get the middle or highest rate of the DLA care component or the daily living component of PIP paid at either rate, and no one gets carer's allowance for looking after you. You do not get the premium if you live with another person aged 18 or over (eg, a friend or parent), unless s/he is separately liable for rent, you only share a bathroom or hallway, or in some other circumstances. See CPAG's *Welfare Benefits and Tax Credits Handbook* for details. If you have a partner, you do not qualify unless your partner also qualifies in her/his own right or is certified as severely sight impaired or blind. If you both qualify, you get two premiums. The rate of the premium is £65.85.

Components

In the main phase (see p24), you receive either the support component or, if your claim began before 3 April 2017, the work-related activity component (see p25). The work-related activity component is £29.05. The support component is £38.55.

Housing costs

ESA can include help with certain service charges and some other housing payments, after a waiting period. Usually help only starts once you have been getting ESA for 39 weeks, although there are some exceptions to this.

If you own your own home, the DWP may offer you a loan to help with the cost of your mortgage interest payments.

Normally you have to live in the home you own to get a loan, but there are exceptions for full-time students (and some others). You can still get a loan for mortgage interest if you have moved elsewhere to study but are not paying rent or a mortgage at the term-time address. If you pay for both places, you can get a loan for both if you are a couple and it is unavoidable that you live in two separate homes. Otherwise, you can get a loan if you are away from your home temporarily and have not let it out and are not likely to be away for more than 52 weeks.[13]
Note: these loans are not part of your ESA.

If you have rent to pay, you must usually claim UC (or sometimes HB) for help (see Chapter 11 or Chapter 6). For full details, see CPAG's *Welfare Benefits and Tax Credits Handbook*.

Chapter 4: Employment and support allowance
7. Other benefits and tax credits

5. Claiming employment and support allowance

How you claim employment and support allowance (ESA) depends on your circumstances. You start your claim for **contributory** ESA by completing the claim form (see www.gov.uk/employment-support-allowance/how-to-claim). If you are claiming ESA, rather than universal credit, because you qualify for a severe disability premium in another benefit (eg, housing benefit or income support) (see p20), you start your claim by phoning Jobcentre Plus on 0800 169 0350 (textphone 0800 023 4888), or claim on Form ESA1 which you can download from www.gov.uk/employment-support-allowance/how-to-claim.

Either member of a couple can make a claim for income-related ESA for both, but whoever claims must be eligible in her/his own right. You claim contributory ESA for yourself only.

You are usually interviewed after you claim. You must provide medical certificates from your GP until you are assessed under the work capability assessment.

Claims for ESA can be backdated for up to three months.

6. Challenging a decision

If you think a decision about your employment and support allowance is wrong, you can ask the DWP to look at it again. This process is known as a 'mandatory reconsideration'. Provided you ask within the time limit (usually one month), the DWP notifies you of the decision in a 'mandatory reconsideration notice'. If you are still not happy when you get this notice, you can appeal to the independent First-tier Tribunal. If it was not possible to ask the DWP to reconsider the decision within a month, you can ask for a late revision (within 13 months), explaining why it is late. You can also ask the DWP to look at a decision again at any time if certain grounds are met – eg, if there has been an official error.

7. Other benefits and tax credits

You cannot get employment and support allowance (ESA) if you are getting statutory sick pay (SSP) from an employer.[14] SSP runs out after 28 weeks, after which you can claim ESA.

You can claim contributory ESA and have this topped up by universal credit (UC). You cannot get ESA if you are getting income support (IS) or jobseeker's allowance (JSA). You can claim contributory ESA if your partner is getting IS or

29

Chapter 4: Employment and support allowance
Notes

JSA. You are excluded if you get joint-claim JSA.[15] You cannot get income-related ESA if your partner gets UC, IS, income-based JSA or pension credit.

Income-related ESA passports you to maximum housing benefit, free school lunches, budgeting loans, Best Start grants and funeral support payments. It also passports you to free dental treatment, vouchers for glasses, and to Best Start foods if you are pregnant or have a child under three (see Chapters 5 and 14).

If you have a child(ren) and a partner and you get contributory ESA, you may be eligible for working tax credit if your partner works 16 hours or more a week, rather than the usual 24 hours.

ESA is taken into account when calculating whether the benefit cap applies, unless you or your partner get a support component in your ESA. If this is the case, you are exempt from the benefit cap (see p49 and p98).

Notes

1. What is employment and support allowance
1 Reg 1 ESA Regs

2. Who is eligible
2 s1 WRA 2007
3 s1 WRA 2007
4 Sch 1 para 6 WRA 2007
5 Reg 18 ESA Regs
6 Regs 14-16 ESA Regs

3. Limited capability for work
7 Reg 33(2) ESA Regs
8 Regs 54 and 63(1) ESA Regs
9 Reg 14(2A) ESA Regs

4. Amount of benefit
10 s2 WRA 2007; reg 67(2) and (3) ESA Regs
11 s4 WRA 2007; reg 67(1) and (3) ESA Regs
12 Reg 67 and Sch 4 ESA Regs
13 Sch 3 para 4 LMI Regs

7. Other benefits and tax credits
14 s20 WRA 2007
15 s1(3)(f) WRA 2007

Chapter 5

Health benefits

This chapter covers:
1. What are health benefits (below)
2. Who is eligible (below)
3. Claiming health benefits (p35)
4. Challenging a decision (p36)

Basic facts
– Everyone in Scotland is entitled to free NHS eye and dental checks and free prescriptions.
– Full-time students under 19 can get free dental treatment and vouchers for glasses.
– Any student under 18 can get free NHS dental treatment.
– Other students can get help if they have a low income or in certain other circumstances.

1. What are health benefits

There are charges for some NHS treatments and services including:
- glasses and contact lenses;
- dental treatment.

There are also often costs incurred in getting to hospital. You may be exempt from these charges or be able to claim help with them on low income grounds.[1]

There is no charge for NHS eye and dental checks, or for prescriptions. **Note:** if you have an English prescription form there may be a charge, but there are exemptions.[2]

2. Who is eligible

Under age 18

If you are under 18, you are entitled to free NHS dental treatment. It does not matter if you are studying full time or part time, or not studying at all.

Chapter 5: Health benefits
2. Who is eligible

Under age 19

If you are in full-time education, you are entitled to free NHS dental treatment and vouchers for glasses.

If you are in part-time education, you are not automatically exempt from NHS charges, but you might get help because you get a qualifying benefit, are in an exempt group or qualify under the low income scheme (see p33).

Aged 19 or over

You are not automatically exempt from NHS charges because you are a student, but you might get help because you get a qualifying benefit, are in an exempt group or qualify under the low income scheme.

Qualifying benefits

You get free NHS dental treatment, vouchers for glasses and certain fares to hospital if you get:
- universal credit (UC) and you:[3]
  - have no earnings; *or*
  - earn £435 or less a month (or, if you have a partner, your combined earnings are £435 or less a month); *or*
  - have a child element in your UC, or you or your partner (or both of you) have limited capability for work and earn £935 or less a month (or, if you have a partner, your combined earnings are £935 or less a month);
- income support (IS);
- income-based jobseeker's allowance (JSA);
- income-related employment and support allowance (ESA);
- guarantee credit of pension credit (PC);
- child tax credit (CTC) and your income for tax credit purposes is £15,276 or less; *or*
- working tax credit (WTC) with a disabled worker element or severe disability element and your income for tax credit purposes is £15,276 or less.

Exempt groups

Dental treatment

You are eligible for free NHS dental treatment if:
- you are pregnant or have given birth in the last year;
- you are under the Public Dental Service (for people who have difficulty getting treatment for reasons such as a disability);
- you are an asylum seeker getting asylum support;
- you get a war pension and need treatment for your war disablement; *or*
- you are a care leaver getting support from the local authority under section 29 of the Children (Scotland) Act 1995.

Vouchers for glasses or contact lenses

You are eligible for vouchers for glasses if:
- you are aged under 16;
- you have a prescription for complex lenses;
- you are a Hospital Eye Service patient;
- you are an asylum seeker getting asylum support;
- you get a war pension and need treatment for your war disablement; *or*
- you are a care leaver getting support from the local authority under section 29 of the Children (Scotland) Act 1995.

Fares to hospital

You are eligible for help with fares to hospital if:
- it is 30 miles or more away, or involves a journey of five miles or more by sea, and you live in the Highlands or Islands – ie:
  - the Highland region, Western Isles, Orkney Islands, Shetland Islands;
  - Arran, Great Cumbrae, Little Cumbrae;
  - the area formerly covered by Argyll and Bute District Council;
  - parts of Moray (Aberlour, Cabrach, Dallas, Dyke, Edinkillie, Forres, Inveravon, Kinloss, Kirkmichael, Knockando, Mortlach, Rafford, Rothes);
- you are an asylum seeker getting asylum support;
- you get a war pension and need treatment for your war disablement; *or*
- you are a care leaver getting support from the local authority under section 29 of the Children (Scotland) Act 1995.

Low income scheme

If you are on a low income, you may be eligible for help under the low income scheme, even if you do not qualify on other grounds.

Under the low income scheme, your income is worked out in almost the same way as for an IS assessment and compared with your needs in the form of premiums and allowances, as in IS but with certain housing costs added.

Step one: capital

You do not qualify if your capital is over £16,000. If capital is between £6,000.01 and £16,000, add £1 to your income for every £250, or part of £250, between these limits.

Chapter 5: Health benefits
2. Who is eligible

Step two: work out your requirements

This is an amount for basic weekly needs. See Chapter 7 for details of how to qualify for each premium. Your requirements are made up of:
- **personal allowances**

– single person aged under 25	£57.90
– single person aged under 25, entitled to an ESA component or incapable of work for 28 weeks since 27 October 2008	£73.10
– single person aged 25 or over	£73.10
– single person aged 60 or over	£167.25
– lone parent aged under 60	£73.10
– lone parent aged 60 or over	£167.25
– couple both aged under 60	£114.85
– couple one or both aged 60 or over	£255.25

- **premiums**
  - carer (as for IS);
  - disability (as for IS, except that this is included after 28 weeks of incapacity for work, rather than 52 weeks). You also get a disability premium if you (or your partner) are under 60 and get ESA with a work-related activity or support component, or have been getting ESA for at least 28 weeks, or have had limited capability for work for at least 28 weeks since 27 October 2008. The amount of the disability premium increases to £38.55 if you are single or a lone parent and get ESA with the support component, get the disability living allowance middle or highest rate care component or get the standard or enhanced rate of the daily living component of personal independence payment, and have been incapable of work for 28 weeks since 27 October 2008;
  - enhanced disability for an adult (as for IS) and also if you (or your partner) are under 60 and get ESA with a support component;
  - severe disability (as for IS).
- **weekly rent** less any housing benefit (HB) and non-dependant deductions;
- **weekly council tax**, if you are liable, less any council tax reduction;
- **mortgage interest**, endowment payments and capital repayments on your home, as well as on loans to adapt a home for a disabled person, deducting any non-dependant deductions;
- **amounts for children**. If you have children, you are likely to be exempt from charges through getting a qualifying benefit like IS, JSA or CTC (see p32). If you get CTC but are not exempt from charges, your children are not included in the low income assessment.

Step three: work out your weekly income

Income is calculated in a very similar way as it is for IS. Your income is taken into account, as well as the income of your partner. Information about how your income is calculated and how student income is treated is in Chapter 19.

Step four: deduct weekly income from requirements

If your income is less than your requirements or no more than £4.50 (half the cost of an English prescription) higher, you are entitled to maximum help with health benefits. If your income is more than £4.50 higher than your needs, you might get partial help.

You are expected to contribute your 'excess income' (the amount by which your income exceeds your needs) towards hospital fares, and can get help with the rest of the costs up to the maximum amount allowed. You are expected to contribute twice your excess income towards help with glasses or contact lenses and three times your excess income towards help with dental charges.[4]

Examples

Madhu is a second-year undergraduate aged 20. She has a student loan of £5,750 and a young students' bursary of £2,000. She is single, has no children and pays £65 rent a week. She gets no HB. Under the low income scheme, her requirements are £122.90 (£57.90 personal allowance, plus £65 rent). Her income from her student loan is £97.25 (see p168). Her income is below her requirements so she is entitled to free NHS dental treatment and vouchers for glasses.

Lewis is 26 and is a second-year undergraduate. He needs dental treatment costing £90. His weekly income for health benefits is £116.48 student loan, plus £50 earnings, making a total of £166.48 (see p168). His needs are £73.10 personal allowance plus £75 weekly rent, a total of £148.10. His excess income is £18.38. He must contribute £55.14 (three times his excess income) to his dental treatment. The other £34.86 is paid for him under the low income scheme.

3. Claiming health benefits

If you are exempt from charges because you are a student under 19, you are under 18 or because you get a qualifying benefit, you should fill in the form when you go for treatment.

If you need to claim on low income grounds and do not get a qualifying benefit, you should claim in advance on Form HC1. You can get this from surgeries, hospitals, opticians, pharmacies and Jobcentre Plus offices, or you can download a form from the NHS Business Services Authority website at www.nhsbsa.nhs.uk. You must provide details of your student loan, grant or bursary, and include a copy of your award letter.

Chapter 5: Health benefits
Notes

If you have already paid for treatment, claim a refund on Form HC5 within three months.

4. Challenging a decision

If you are claiming under the low income scheme, you can ask for a formal review of the decision on your claim by writing to the NHS Business Services Authority, Bridge House, 152 Pilgrim Street, Newcastle upon Tyne NE1 6SN, or online at www.nhsbsa.nhs.uk.

Notes

1. What are health benefits
1 NHS(TERC)(S) Regs, as amended (most recently in 2015 by SI No.333); The National Health Service (Optical Charges and Payments) (Scotland) Regulations 1998, No.642, as amended (most recently in 2019 by SI No.50); The National Health Service (Free Prescriptions and Charges for Drugs and Appliances) (Scotland) Regulations 2011, No.55, as amended (most recently in 2019 by SI No.145); The National Health Service (Dental Charges) (Scotland) Regulations 2003, No.158, as amended (most recently in 2011 by SI No.168)
2 Reg 4 The National Health Service (Free Prescriptions and Charges for Drugs and Appliances) (Scotland) Regulations 2011, No.55, as amended (most recently in 2019 by SI No.145)

2. Who is eligible
3 The NHS (Payments and Remission of Charges) (Miscellaneous Amendments) (Scotland) Regulations 2017, No.59
4 Reg 5 NHS(TERC)(S) Regs, as amended (most recently in 2015 by SI No.333); regs 14 and 19 The National Health Service (Optical Charges and Payments) (Scotland) Regulations 1998, No.642, as amended (most recently in 2019 by SI No.50)

Chapter 6

Housing benefit

This chapter covers:
1. What is housing benefit (below)
2. Who is eligible (p38)
3. Basic rules (p40)
4. Amount of benefit (p43)
5. Claiming housing benefit (p48)
6. Challenging a decision (p48)
7. Other benefits and tax credits (p49)

> **Basic facts**
> – Housing benefit (HB) helps with your rent.
> – It is administered by local authorities.
> – Full-time students are eligible if they are on a non-advanced course and are under 21 (or are 21 and turned 21 on their course).
> – Other full-time students are eligible if they get income support, income-based jobseeker's allowance or income-related employment and support allowance, or if they are a lone parent, disabled or over pension age.
> – Couples with a child are eligible throughout the year, whether one or both are students.
> – There are limits to the rent covered by HB.
> – HB is means tested and the amount you get depends on your grant, loan and other income.

1. What is housing benefit

Housing benefit (HB) helps with your rent. Most full-time students are not eligible, but part-time students are. You can get help with rent in private accommodation, but not if you live with your parents. There are limits to the level of rent that HB covers. HB is means tested, so your grant, loan and other income affect the amount you get.

Note: people under pension age cannot usually make a new claim for HB, as it is being replaced by universal credit (UC). However an exception applies if:

- you have a severe disability premium in your income support, income-based jobseeker's allowance, income-related employment support allowance or HB (or you got one in the past month and you continue to satisfy the rules for it); or
- you live in certain types of specified or temporary accommodation, such as homeless accommodation (you may still need to claim UC as well for your living costs). See CPAG's *Welfare Benefits and Tax Credits Handbook* for details.

2. Who is eligible

To qualify for housing benefit (HB), you must be a student who is eligible to get HB (see below), your accommodation must be eligible for HB (see p42) and you must satisfy the basic HB rules (see p40). As new claims cannot usually be made (see p37 for exceptions), most students getting HB will be those who were already on HB before starting the course, and who are eligible for HB as a student. If you cannot claim HB, you may be able to get help with your rent through universal credit (see Chapter 11).

Full-time students

If you are a full-time student 'attending or undertaking a full-time course of study', you cannot normally get HB.[1] However, there are exceptions for some students.

You start being a student from the first day you attend or undertake the course. You stop being a student after the last day of the final academic term in which you are enrolled, or from the day you finally abandon your course or are dismissed from it.[2]

Who counts as a full-time student

In most cases you are treated as a full-time student if your college or university says your course is full time.

If you are at a further education (FE) college, not on a higher education course, and your course is government funded, a learning agreement from the college shows how many hours are involved in the course and a 16/21-hour rule determines whether it is full or part time.[3] The rules on whether or not you count as a full-time student are the same as for income support (IS), except that there is no 12-hour rule if you are claiming HB and are aged under 20 and in relevant education. In this case, the 16/21-hour rule applies (see p55).

Guidance states that postgraduates stop being treated as full-time students for HB purposes when their course ends. If you go on to do further research or write up a thesis, whether or not you are regarded as full time depends on how much work you are doing at the time, not on whether the course is full time.[4]

Chapter 6: Housing benefit
2. Who is eligible

Who can get housing benefit

You are eligible for HB as a full-time student if you are in one of the following groups.[5]

- You are under 21 on a full-time course of non-advanced education (see p52) (benefit can continue if you turn 21 on your course, but stops once you turn 22), or you are a child or qualifying young person for child benefit purposes (see Chapter 2), even if no one gets child benefit for you.[6] **Note:** if you are a care leaver and are aged 16 or 17, you cannot get HB, even if you come into one of the groups below, because the local authority should be supporting you.
- You are on IS, income-based jobseeker's allowance (JSA) or income-related employment and support allowance (ESA).
- You are a lone parent of a child under 16, or under 20 if s/he is still a qualifying young person (see p9). Lone parents can only usually get IS until their youngest child's fifth birthday (see p57). If your IS stops, make sure you tell the local authority that pays your HB.
- You or your partner have reached pension age. Pension age reached 65 in November 2018 and is due to reach 66 by October 2020. For more details, see *CPAG's Welfare Benefits and Tax Credits Handbook*.
- You qualify for a disability premium or severe disability premium with your HB – eg, you get disability living allowance (DLA), personal independence payment or long-term incapacity benefit (IB), or are certified as severely sight impaired or blind. See pp63–64 for details. **Note:** you cannot qualify for a disability premium if you have limited capability for work.[7]
- You have been incapable of work for the last 28 weeks. Since 27 October 2008, new claimants are assessed under the limited capability for work test (see below). However, the previous incapacity for work test may still apply to you if you are already getting IB, or IS on the basis of disability.
- You have had limited capability for work for the last 28 weeks and you continue to have limited capability for work. You should claim ESA to have your limited capability for work acknowledged (although you do not have to get any ESA to qualify). You can add together weeks of limited capability for work on either side of a gap of up to 12 weeks.
- You get a disabled students' allowance because of deafness. You are eligible for HB from the date you apply for the allowance.[8] However, if you are still waiting to hear about the allowance, the local authority may postpone making a decision on your HB claim, but should then fully backdate your benefit.[9]
- You are in a couple, your partner is also a full-time student and you have a dependent child under 16, or under 20 if s/he is a qualifying young person (see p9). Unlike IS and JSA, which you can only claim in the summer vacation, you can claim HB throughout the academic year. If you are claiming IS or income-based JSA, remember that if these benefits stop at the end of the summer vacation, you must tell the local authority so it can reassess your HB. If your

39

partner is not a student, s/he can claim HB for both of you, whether or not you have a child.
- You are single and caring for a child boarded out with you by the social work department.

Studying part time

You can get HB throughout your studies. You must meet all the basic rules below, including being liable for rent and being in eligible accommodation. You are a part-time student if you do not count as a full-time student under the definition on p55. The rules on who counts as full time are the same as those for IS, with one exception. If you are under 20 and in 'relevant education', there is no 12-hour rule. The 16/21-hour rule applies to you if you are on a non-advanced course, whatever your age.

3. Basic rules

As well as being a student who is eligible to claim housing benefit (HB – see p39), you must also meet all the following conditions to qualify.
- You are liable to pay rent (see below).
- You pay rent for the home in which you normally live (see p41).
- Your accommodation is eligible for HB (see p42).
- You satisfy the 'habitual residence' and 'right to reside' tests, and are not a 'person subject to immigration control'. These terms are explained in CPAG's *Welfare Benefits and Tax Credits Handbook*. Overseas students can get further advice from UKCISA (see Appendix 2).
- You have no more than £16,000 capital. There is no capital limit if you are getting pension credit (PC) guarantee credit.
- Your income is sufficiently low (see Chapter 17).

What follows is a brief outline of the basic HB rules, including those that refer specifically to students. For more details, see CPAG's *Welfare Benefits and Tax Credits Handbook*.

Liable for rent

You must be liable for rent. If you are jointly liable for the rent with others (eg, you have each signed the tenancy agreement), the amount of HB you get is based on your share of the rent (although, less commonly, it may not be an equal share if that seems reasonable to the local authority).

If you are in a couple, it does not matter whose name is on the rent agreement; either of you can claim. So if you are a student who is eligible for HB, you can claim for both of you, or if you are not eligible for HB, your non-student partner can claim for both of you.

There are some circumstances in which a local authority has the discretion to treat you as liable for the rent even when you are not legally liable – eg, if you have taken over paying the rent from someone else.

Your normal home

Usually, you can only get HB for one home and that is the place where you normally live. If you are away from your normal home, in some cases your HB may stop. In other cases, you can get HB for two homes at the same time.

You are away from your term-time home

In the summer vacation, you cannot get HB for any weeks you are away from your term-time home, unless you would live there even if you were not studying. To continue to get HB for weeks of absence, you need to argue that your main purpose for living there is not simply to make it easier to attend the course – eg, you were settled there before the course or you are independent of, or estranged from, your parents.[10] However, if your grant or loan covers the summer vacation, your HB does not stop during any weeks of absence.[11] HB does not stop if you have to go into hospital.

If you leave your home during the academic year (or at any time if you live there not just to facilitate attending your course), your HB does not stop, provided you intend to return, you do not sublet, and you are not likely to be away for more than 52 weeks.[12] You cannot use this provision if you can get HB under the 'two homes rule' described below. The two homes rule is, however, more generous because it does not have a time limit.

Examples
John flatshares in Dundee while attending university. He gets HB as a disabled student. During the summer vacation he goes home to stay with his parents in Arbroath for seven weeks. His HB stops and on his return he has to claim universal credit.

Donna has always lived in Ayr and is attending her local college. She is a lone parent and gets HB. She regularly visits her family in Arran during vacations. Her HB continues during her absence.

You have two homes

If you live in one home so that you can attend your course and in another home at other times, but you are only liable for rent on one, you can get HB for that place even while you are not there. This rule applies to lone parents and single students eligible for HB. It does not help you if you pay rent at one place and a mortgage on the other.[13]

> **Example**
> Emily's normal home is in Stornoway, where she lives with her 17-year-old daughter who is at school. She has to pay rent for her Stornoway home. Emily is studying at the University of Glasgow and lives with a cousin rent free while in Glasgow. Emily can get HB for her Stornoway home throughout the year. Whether any HB is payable, and at what times, depends on the amount of her grant and loan.

A couple (one of whom is a student eligible for HB) who have to live in two separate homes can get HB on both if the local authority decides that this is reasonable.[14]

Eligible accommodation

You can get HB to help pay the rent – eg, to a private landlord, local authority, housing association, co-operative or on a croft. It is not essential for you to have a written tenancy agreement; it could be verbal. In some circumstances you cannot get HB – eg, if:[15]
- you live with and pay rent to your parents, a sister or brother, or a son or daughter (including in-laws, partners and step-relatives);
- you pay rent to someone (who might be a relative or friend), but your tenancy is not on a commercial basis. This rule often prevents people getting HB if they live in a property owned by their parents. It is possible, however, to get HB in these circumstances if the tenancy is a commercial one. If this applies to you, get advice;
- your tenancy was contrived in order to try to get HB;
- you pay rent to an ex-partner with whom you used to share the home in which you now live.

Halls of residence

You can get HB for rent in a student hall of residence.[16] You must be a full-time student who is eligible for HB (see p39). You cannot get HB in a hall if you are claiming while waiting to return to your course after taking time out because of disability, illness or caring responsibilities.

Part-time students can also get HB in a hall of residence if, had they been full time, they would have been eligible to claim HB as:
- an under-22-year-old in non-advanced education;
- a lone parent;
- a disabled student;

- someone with a child and a full-time student partner; *or*
- someone who has reached pension age (see p39).

If you get income support (IS), income-based jobseeker's allowance (JSA) or income-related employment and support allowance (ESA) as a part-time student, you can only get HB in a hall of residence if you are also one of the above. Although you can get HB, it might not cover the whole cost (see below).

Full-time students waiting to return to their course after a period of illness or caring, and part-time students on IS, income-based JSA or income-related ESA, and not in another category cannot get HB in a hall of residence during term time or short vacations unless the educational establishment does not own the hall, does not have a long-term lease on the building or does not rent it from the education authority.[17] For example, if the university leases flats on a short-term lease from a private landlord and rents these to students, you can get HB. During the summer vacation, you can get HB if you remain in the hall, unless your student support covers the summer vacation.

4. Amount of benefit

The amount of housing benefit (HB) you get depends on the maximum rent the local authority is prepared to pay, and on your income compared with the amount the law says you need to live on. The amount you get may be reduced if your total income from benefits and tax credits is above a certain level (see p49). To work out your HB, go through the following steps.

Step one: capital

If your capital is over £16,000, you cannot get HB unless you are over pension age and get pension credit (PC) guarantee credit (see p157). Some kinds of capital are ignored. For details, see CPAG's *Welfare Benefits and Tax Credits Handbook*.

Step two: maximum rent

There is a maximum amount of rent the local authority is prepared to cover. This might be less than the actual amount of rent you pay – eg, if you pay service charges that are not covered by HB (see p44), or if your rent for HB purposes is reduced because you have a spare bedroom (see p44).

HB does not cover some items included in rent, such as charges for:
- water or sewerage;
- fuel. Either the actual charge specified in the rental agreement or a fixed rate is deducted;
- meals. If these are included in your rent, the local authority may deduct a fixed rate;

Chapter 6: Housing benefit
4. Amount of benefit

- services. Some are included (eg, cleaning communal areas, provision of a laundry room and TV signal relay, including free-to-view TV but not an individual satellite dish or set-top box) and others are not – eg, sports facilities and TV rental.

See CPAG's *Welfare Benefits and Tax Credits Handbook* for details of the deductions.

If you rent from a private landlord (including a hall of residence) and you claimed HB or moved home on or after 7 April 2008, your HB is based on a 'standard local housing allowance' for the size of property that applies to you, even if your rent is higher than this amount. If your rent is lower, HB is based on the amount of your actual rent. Each local authority has its own rates for properties of different sizes. Check your local authority's rates at http://lha-direct.voa.gov.uk/search.aspx.

Generally, unless you are a single person aged under 35, you are allowed one bedroom for:
- an adult couple;
- another single adult aged 16 or over;
- two children under 16 of the same sex;
- two children under 10;
- any other child.

You are allowed a maximum of four bedrooms. If you are a single person under 35, you usually only get a lower, shared-accommodation rate. If you are disabled and need overnight care, you may qualify for an additional bedroom for a carer. See CPAG's *Welfare Benefits and Tax Credits Handbook* for details.

If the local housing allowance rules do not apply, your case is usually referred to a rent officer to decide how much help with rent you should get, based on other local rents. For details of these 'local reference rent' rules, see CPAG's *Welfare Benefits and Tax Credits Handbook*.

If you rent from a local authority or housing association, your maximum rent is usually the same as the weekly rent due less any of the above ineligible charges. However, your HB is reduced if you are considered to have a spare bedroom (known as the 'bedroom tax'). The rules about how many bedrooms you can have are similar to the local housing allowance rules, but see CPAG's *Welfare Benefits and Tax Credits Handbook* for more information. If you are considered to have one spare bedroom, your maximum rent is reduced by 14 per cent and by 25 per cent if you have two spare bedrooms. If your HB is reduced in this way, you should apply for a discretionary housing payment from the local authority (see below).

Discretionary housing payments

If your HB does not cover your rent, you may be able to get a discretionary housing payment from your local authority. These can be paid if you get HB and need additional help with your housing costs – eg, to make up the shortfall in rent due to HB being reduced because you have a spare bedroom. They are usually awarded for a temporary period, beyond which you have to reapply.

Step three: deductions for non-dependants

An amount is deducted from your maximum rent if you have a 'non-dependant' living with you.

A 'non-dependant' is someone, usually a friend or adult relative, who lives with you but not on a commercial basis. A deduction is made to reflect an assumed contribution from her/him to the household, whether or not s/he pays anything. There is no deduction for:[18]
- a full-time student during the academic year (whether or not s/he works);
- a full-time student during the summer vacation (but there is a deduction if s/he starts working 16 hours or more a week unless her/his student support covers the summer vacation);
- a full-time student at any time if you or your partner have reached pension age;
- a joint occupier or joint tenant;
- a resident landlord;
- a sub-tenant;
- your partner or dependent child;
- anyone under 18;
- anyone under 25 if s/he gets universal credit (UC), provided s/he does not have any earned income for UC purposes, or if s/he gets income support (IS), income-based jobseeker's allowance (JSA), income-related employment and support allowance (ESA) without a work-related activity component (or who is not in the 'work-related activity group') or support component (this usually only applies in the first 13 weeks of an ESA claim);
- someone who gets a youth training allowance;
- someone who normally lives elsewhere;
- someone in hospital for more than 52 weeks, or in prison;
- a live-in paid carer from a voluntary organisation;
- someone on PC.

No deductions are made for your non-dependants if you or your partner are registered blind, get the disability living allowance care component, personal independence payment daily living component or attendance allowance.

For anyone else, fixed deductions are made based on the non-dependant's income. See CPAG's *Welfare Benefits and Tax Credits Handbook* for details and amounts. **Note:** if your non-dependant is working, you should provide the local authority with evidence of her/his gross income. If you do not, the local authority may make the highest deduction.

If you or your partner have reached pension age and do not get IS, income-based JSA, income-related ESA or UC, the deduction is not made until 26 weeks

Chapter 6: Housing benefit
4. Amount of benefit

after the non-dependant moves in with you. Likewise if her/his income goes up, increasing the deduction, the increased deduction does not take effect for 26 weeks.

Step four: getting a means-tested benefit

If you get IS, income-based JSA, income-related ESA, UC or PC, HB is the amount worked out at Step three – ie, your maximum rent less any amount for non-dependants. In this case, you do not need to continue with the rest of these steps.

Step five: not getting a means-tested benefit

If you do not get IS, income-based JSA, income-related ESA, UC or PC, you must compare your income with your weekly needs.

Step six: work out your applicable amount

This is an amount for your basic weekly needs. It is made up of:
- personal allowances;
- premiums;
- a work-related activity or support component if you have limited capability for work.

The applicable amount includes amounts for yourself and for your partner, if you have one. It also includes amounts for any dependent children. The amounts for HB are the same as for IS (see p61), but with the following differences.

- **Personal allowance:**
  - a child allowance is included in HB;
  - single people under 25 and lone parents under 18 who are entitled to main phase ESA get £73.10;
  - young couples get £114.85, unless both are under 18 and the claimant is not entitled to main phase ESA (see p24), in which case they get £87.50;
  - single people have a personal allowance of £181 if they have reached pension age (see p39);
  - couples get £270.60 if one or both has reached pension age (see p39), and they do not get IS, income-based JSA, income-related ESA or UC.
- **Premiums:**
  - a family premium is included in your HB if you already have an existing claim which includes a child. It is not included in an existing claim if you later have a child, or in new claims from 1 May 2016;
  - a disabled child premium and enhanced disability premium for a child are included in HB;
  - you do not get a disability premium if you have been assessed as having limited capability for work for ESA and you (ie, not your partner) are the HB claimant.

Chapter 6: Housing benefit
4. Amount of benefit

- Components:
  - instead of a disability premium, a work-related activity component of £29.05 is included if you claimed ESA before 3 April 2017 and have limited capability for work, or a support component of £38.55 is included if you have limited capability for work-related activity (see p28).

Step seven: work out your weekly income

Chapter 17 explains how your loan, grant or other income is taken into account and how to work out your weekly income.

Step eight: calculate your housing benefit

If your income is *less than or the same as* your applicable amount, HB is the amount worked out at Step three – ie, your maximum rent less any amounts for non-dependants.

If your income is *more than* your applicable amount, work out 65 per cent of the difference. Your HB is the amount worked out at Step three (ie, your maximum rent less any amounts for non-dependants) minus 65 per cent of the difference between your income and applicable amount.

Example
Maria is 18 and studying full time for a National Certificate in animal care. Her course lasts for one year (40 weeks in total). She shares a private-rented flat with a friend. They each pay £70 a week rent. She has a bursary maintenance allowance of £4,186 per year. The local housing allowance shared accommodation rate in her area is £60 a week (her maximum rent for HB).

	£
Maximum rent	60.00
Applicable amount	57.90
Income (bursary)	4,186
Less (books and equipment)	390.00
Less (travel)	303.00
Equals	3,493
Divided by 40 weeks for weekly income	87.33
Subtract applicable amount from income (£87.33 – £57.90)	29.43
Calculate 65 per cent of the difference	19.13
Deduct from maximum rent (£60) to give weekly HB	**40.87**

Maria can get HB of £40.87 per week during her course.

5. Claiming housing benefit

If you can still make a claim for housing benefit (HB) (see p37), you can get a claim form from your local authority HB office. You may also be able to claim online. If you return the form to your local HB office, ask for a receipt. If you return it by post, keep a copy, as claim forms are often lost. If you need to fill in another form, the local authority can backdate it if you can show the date of your original claim.

If you are also claiming income support (IS), income-based jobseeker's allowance (JSA), employment and support allowance (ESA) or pension credit (PC), you may be able to claim HB at the same time. The DWP should either take your claim over the phone or give you a form, usually Form HCTB1.

When your housing benefit starts

Your HB starts from when you make your claim. It can be backdated for up to one month if you ask for this and you have continuous 'good cause' for not claiming throughout the whole period. When deciding whether there is good cause to backdate a claim, a local authority must take into account how a reasonable person of your age, experience and state of health would have acted or failed to act in the same circumstances.[19] If you have reached pension age (see p39) and are not on IS, income-based JSA or income-related ESA, HB can be backdated for up to three months whatever the reason for the delay.

HB is usually paid directly into your rent account if you are a council tenant, otherwise it is either paid to you or directly to your landlord.

By law, local authorities are supposed to pay you within 14 days of receiving your completed claim form or as soon as possible after that. However, in many areas there are long delays. If you are a private tenant, ask for a **'payment on account'** until your claim can be properly assessed. Local authorities are legally obliged to give you an interim payment of a reasonable amount, unless it is obvious that you will not be entitled to HB or you have not supplied information that has been requested.

6. Challenging a decision

If you think a decision about your housing benefit is wrong (eg, because the decision maker got the facts or law wrong), there are a number of ways you can try to get the decision changed.

- You can ask for the decision to be looked at again (known as a 'revision' or a 'supersession'). In some cases, you must show specific grounds. In others, you must apply within a strict time limit, usually one month.

You can appeal to the independent First-tier Tribunal. There are strict time limits for appealing – usually one month from the date you are sent the decision. You can make a late appeal in limited circumstances.

If you are considering challenging a decision, get advice as soon as possible.

7. Other benefits and tax credits

Child tax credit (CTC) counts in full as income when housing benefit (HB) is worked out. It is the actual amount you are paid that counts. If your CTC award is reduced because an overpayment of tax credit is being recovered, it is the reduced amount that counts for HB. If you are underpaid CTC and get a lump-sum repayment, this is treated as capital for HB, so it only affects your HB if it takes your savings above the capital limit. The rules are the same for working tax credit (WTC).

Child benefit is disregarded as income for HB.

Bear in mind that you should tell the local authority about any changes in income when they occur, including benefit and tax credit changes. Do not assume that the DWP or HM Revenue and Customs passes on the information for you.

The benefit cap

Your HB is reduced if your total income from benefits is over the maximum amount that you or your partner can receive. The amount is £384.62 a week if you are a lone parent or member of a couple, and £257.69 if you are a single person.

Most benefits count towards the cap, including income support, jobseeker's allowance, employment and support allowance (ESA), child benefit, CTC and HB. The cap also applies to universal credit (see p98).

You are exempt from the cap if you or your partner are working, or if you are disabled, a carer or a war widow(er). To count as working, you must get WTC. You are exempt from the cap because of disability if you or your partner get certain disability benefits, including disability living allowance (DLA), personal independence payment (PIP) and ESA with a support component. You are also exempt if a child or young person for whom you are responsible gets DLA or PIP. You are exempt if you or your partner get carer's allowance.

There is protection for nine months before the cap applies if you are no longer working but were working at least 16 hours a week for the last year.

Passported benefits

Provided you meet any other conditions, getting HB entitles you to:
- a Best Start grant;
- Best Start foods;

Chapter 6: Housing benefit
Notes

- funeral support payments (provided income for HB purposes is below £311 a week).

Notes

2. Who is eligible
1. Regs 53(1), definition of 'full-time student', and 56(1) HB Regs
2. Reg 53(1), definition of 'last day of the course', and (2)(b) HB Regs
3. Reg 53(1), definition of 'full-time course of study', HB Regs
4. para 2.354 C2 GM
5. Reg 56(2) HB Regs
6. Reg 56(2)(h) HB Regs
7. Sch 3 paras 12 and 13(9) HB Regs
8. Reg 56(2)(i) HB Regs
9. para 2.30 C2 GM

3. Basic rules
10. Reg 55 HB Regs
11. Regs 53(1), definition of 'period of study', and 55 HB Regs
12. Reg 7(16)(c)(viii) HB Regs
13. Reg 7(3) HB Regs
14. Reg 7(6)(b) HB Regs
15. Reg 9 HB Regs
16. Reg 57(4) HB Regs
17. Reg 57(2) HB Regs

4. Amount of benefit
18. Regs 3 and 74 HB Regs

5. Claiming housing benefit
19. Reg 83(12) HB Regs; R(S) 2/63(T)

Chapter 7

Income support

This chapter covers:
1. What is income support (below)
2. Who is eligible (p52)
3. Basic rules (p60)
4. Amount of benefit (p60)
5. Claiming income support (p64)
6. Challenging a decision (p65)
7. Other benefits and tax credits (p65)

Basic facts
– Income support provides basic financial support for people who are not expected to 'sign on' for work.
– Part-time students are eligible if they are a lone parent with a child under five, a carer, pregnant (and sick or nearly due), and in some other circumstances.
– Full-time students under 20 on non-advanced courses may be eligible if they are a parent, an orphan or estranged or separated from their parents, and in some other circumstances.
– Other full-time students are eligible if they are a lone parent with a child under five, and in some other circumstances.
– The amount is usually affected by any grant, loan or other income you may have.

1. What is income support

Income support (IS) provides basic financial support for people under pension age (see p60) who are not expected to 'sign on' as available for work. Students who are lone parents with a child under five may be eligible for IS, as may some younger students on non-advanced courses who are estranged from their parents or who are parents themselves. Most other full-time students are not eligible. See p52 for which students can get IS.

Note: you cannot usually make a new claim for IS as it is in the process of being replaced by universal credit. However, an exception applies if you get, or got in

Chapter 7: Income support
2. Who is eligible

the past month (and continue to satisfy the rules for it), a severe disability premium in your IS, income-based jobseeker's allowance, income-related employment and support allowance or housing benefit.

The amount you get is based on your circumstances – eg, whether you have a partner or whether you (or your partner) have a disability or care for someone with a disability. The amount you get is usually affected by any grant, loan or other income you have.

2. Who is eligible

As new claims cannot usually be made (see p51 for exceptions), most students getting income support (IS) will be those who were already on IS before starting the course, and who are eligible for IS as a student. If you cannot claim IS, you may be able to get universal credit (UC) instead – eg, if you are a parent (see Chapter 11).

To qualify for IS, you must be in one of the groups eligible to claim and you must satisfy all the basic rules described on p60.

Only certain groups of students are eligible for IS, depending on your age and your course. To check whether you can get IS if you are:
- under 20 and in 'relevant education', see below; *or*
- 19 or over and a full-time student, unless you are aged 19 and count as being in relevant education, see p55; *or*
- under 19 in full-time advanced education, see p58; *or*
- studying part time, see p58.

Under 20 in relevant education

Generally, you cannot get IS if you are under 20 and in 'relevant education', but there are exceptions.[1]

What is relevant education

You count as being in relevant education if you are a 'qualifying young person' for child benefit purposes (see p9) – ie, you are 19 or under and attending a full-time course of non-advanced education or an approved training course (see p9) which you were accepted on, enrolled on or started when you were under 19.[2] If you are accepted on, enrol on or start a full-time course of non-advanced education on or after your 19th birthday, you are not in relevant education. The rules on p55 apply to you instead.

> *Full-time non-advanced education*
> Your course is classed as **'full time'** for IS purposes if it is for more than 12 hours a week during term time. These 12 hours include classes and supervised study, but not meal breaks or unsupervised study either at home or at college.[3]

Chapter 7: Income support
2. Who is eligible

'**Non-advanced education**' is anything below degree, Higher National Certificate (HNC) or Higher National Diploma (HND) level, and includes school-level courses.

Non-advanced courses	Advanced courses
National Qualifications (NQ) Nationals 1 to 5	HNC
NQ Higher or Advanced Higher	HND
Scottish Vocational Qualification (SVQ) levels 1–3	SVQ level 4 or 5
National Progression Awards	Degree level
National Certificate	Postgraduate
Scottish Wider Access Programme	

You may still count as being in relevant education for a period after your course ends (see p54).

Who can get income support

If you are aged 16, 17, 18 (or, in some cases, 19 – see p52), and in relevant education, you are eligible for IS if you are in one of the following groups.[4]

- You are an orphan and no one is acting in place of your parent. You do not qualify if, for example, you are living with a foster parent or being looked after by the local authority.
- You must live away from your parents or anyone acting in their place because you are estranged from them. Decision makers should believe you if you say you are estranged unless there is valid evidence that this may not be the case.[5] If a decision maker questions what you say, s/he may, with your permission, seek further evidence.[6] It is possible to be estranged from a parent even if you do not both feel the same way about it.[7]
- You must live away from your parents because there is a serious risk to your physical or mental health, or because you are in physical or moral danger. Decision makers are advised to accept your own evidence of physical or moral danger unless there is stronger evidence to the contrary.[8]
- You are living away from your parents and anyone acting in their place, they cannot support you financially, and:
  – they are chronically sick or physically or mentally disabled; *or*
  – they are in prison; *or*
  – they are not allowed to enter Britain.
- You are a parent and your child lives with you.
- You are a refugee learning English in certain circumstances (see p58).
- You have left local authority care and you have to live away from your parents or anyone acting in their place. However, 16/17-year-old care leavers normally get financial support from the local authority social work department, and you cannot get IS in relevant education unless you are a lone parent.[9]

Chapter 7: Income support
2. Who is eligible

Examples

Pete is 17 and studying cookery full time leading to a National Certificate. His father is in prison and his mother is chronically ill. Neither of them can support him financially and he does not live with them. He is eligible for IS.

Ginny is 18 and studying information technology for a National Certificate. She is the mother of a two-year-old child and they both live with Ginny's parents. She is eligible for IS.

Ahmed is 18 and studying full time for Highers. He is a refugee whose parents live in Somalia. It would be dangerous for him to return home. Ahmed is eligible for IS.

Kelly is 16 and studying full time for Highers. She has lived on her own since her father told her to leave home. She is estranged from both her parents. She is eligible for IS.

Laurie is 17 and has left local authority care. She is undertaking a full-time SVQ in beauty therapy. She is a lone parent and so is not excluded from IS as a 16/17-year-old care leaver.

Once you reach your 20th birthday, you are no longer classed as being in 'relevant education' and cannot get IS under these rules. You may be able to continue to get IS as a full-time or part-time student, but only if you are in one of those groups who are eligible (see p56 and p58).

In particular, your claim for IS may be able to continue if you are under 22 on a non-advanced course and without parental support – ie, you are in one of the first four groups in the list on p53.

If you cannot get IS, you may be able to claim UC instead. Otherwise, you may need to contact your college for discretionary financial assistance.

Parents claiming for you

If you are in relevant education but are not in any of the above groups, you cannot get IS. Your parents may be able to get child benefit and UC (or child tax credit (CTC)) for you (see Chapters 2 and 12).

If you get IS for yourself, the amount of your parents' benefit may reduce, as:
- any child benefit, UC or CTC they get for you stops;
- any IS or income-based JSA they get for you stops;[10]
- any working tax credit they get stops, unless there are other dependent children in the family or they qualify in another way.

When a course ends

You count as being in relevant education if you have finished a course of non-advanced education and are enrolled or accepted on another such course.[11] This means you are still in relevant education during the summer vacation between courses. Otherwise, you still count as being in relevant education when you finish a course until the latest of the following dates, or until you turn 20 if that is earlier:
- 31 August after your 16th birthday;[12]

- for 16/17-year-olds, 20 weeks after your course ends if you are registered with Skills Development Scotland. This is the 'extension period' rule in child benefit (see p10). **Note:** if you are an orphan, estranged from your parents, living away from your parents because of a risk to your health or because they cannot support you financially, or a care leaver, the requirement that someone must have received child benefit for you immediately before the period started does not apply;[13]
- the last day in February, May, August or November following the date the course ends (an exception allows some young people finishing Highers in May to count as being in relevant education until the end of August).[14]

19 or over and a full-time student

If you are a full-time student aged 19 or over, whether in non-advanced or advanced education, you cannot usually get IS during your 'period of study', but there are exceptions.[15] If you are aged 19 and in relevant education, you come under the rules above.

Period of study

The '**period of study**' starts on the first day of the course and ends on the last day of the course – ie, the last day of the final academic year.[16] It only ends earlier than this if you abandon your course or are dismissed from it, in which case it ends on the day that happens. You are within your period of study during all vacations and, for sandwich courses, during periods of work placements. In your first year, you do not count as a student at all until you first start attending or undertaking the course.[17] So if the course has already begun, you are not excluded from IS as a student until the day you actually start.

Who counts as a full-time student

You count as a '**full-time student**' if you are 'attending or undertaking a full-time course of study at an educational establishment'.[18] There are two definitions of 'full time' that apply: the first covers mostly courses of advanced education; the second covers most courses of non-advanced education.
- **Advanced education.** Your course is full time if it is classed as full time by the institution. If the institution describes the course as full time, you need convincing evidence to persuade the DWP otherwise, bearing in mind that what matters is the course itself rather than the hours you attend.[19] This definition covers all courses of advanced education funded, in whole or in part, by the Scottish government, and any courses of non-advanced education that are not wholly or partly funded by the Scottish government at a further education (FE) college.
- **Non-advanced education.** Your course is full time if it involves more than 16 hours a week classroom or workshop learning under the direct guidance of

Chapter 7: Income support
2. Who is eligible

teaching staff, or 16 hours or less if your hours are made up of more than 21 hours a week of structured study hours.[20] What matters is the number of hours specified in a document signed by the college. This is often called a 'learning agreement', but your college may refer to it by some other name. This definition applies if you are at an FE college, not undertaking a higher education course and your course is fully or partly funded by the Scottish government. Courses funded by the Scottish government include school qualifications like NQs from Access level to Advanced Higher, SVQs and National Certificates.

Sandwich courses

You count as a full-time student if you are on a sandwich course. A **'sandwich course'** is made up of alternate periods of work experience and full-time study at college or university, where the study periods add up to at least 18 weeks in the year.[21]

Work experience includes periods of employment abroad for modern language students whose course is at least half composed of modern language study.

Initial teacher training courses are not treated as sandwich courses.

Modular courses

A **'modular course'** is one that is made up of two or more modules and you are required to do a certain number to complete the course.[22] If you are attending or undertaking part of a modular course that is full time according to the rules described above, you are regarded as being a full-time student for the duration of that module, from the day it begins until the last day of registration on the module (or earlier if you abandon the course or are dismissed from it). This includes all vacations during the module on which you are registered and, except for the final module, the vacation immediately following it. It also includes periods when you are attending the course to do re-sits. If the modular course allows you to undertake some modules on a part-time basis, you are not excluded from IS while you are studying part time.

Postgraduates

If you are a postgraduate, the law is not clear on whether you still count as a student during the period at the end of your course when you are writing up your thesis. DWP guidance says someone is 'not a full-time student during the period after the end of the course when they are expected to complete any course work'.[23] If you are refused IS, consider appealing. You could try arguing that you are no longer attending or undertaking a course.

Who can get income support

You can get IS if you are:[24]
- a lone parent (see p57);

- a single foster parent (see below);
- in a couple, your partner is also a full-time student and you have a child (but you can only get IS in the long vacation – see below);
- a refugee learning English (see p58);
- on a non-advanced course, under 22 and without parental support (see p58).

Lone parents

To qualify as a lone parent, your youngest child must normally be under age five (you can also qualify if you are under 18, regardless of your youngest child's age).[25] Once your youngest child reaches her/his fifth birthday, you no longer count as a lone parent and your IS stops.

> *Examples*
>
> Julie is studying full time for a degree in chemistry. She is a lone parent with a three-year-old child. She is eligible for IS.
>
> Anne is a lone parent with a 14-year-old daughter who has a disability. Anne is a full-time student on a four-year degree course and gets housing benefit which includes a severe disability premium. She is not eligible for IS as a lone parent, but is eligible as a carer in the summer vacation only.

You may be required to attend work-focused interviews if your youngest child is aged one to four, and to undertake work-related activity if your youngest child is aged three or four.

If you are a lone parent and your child is above the age at which you count as a lone parent for IS, but is under 20 and a qualifying young person (see p9), in certain circumstances you can get IS during the summer vacation. You must be in one of the other groups of people who are eligible for IS, such as a carer (see p58), and you must be eligible to make a new claim for IS (see p51).

Single foster parents

You are eligible if you are a single foster parent with a child under 16. This includes kinship carers who are caring for a 'looked-after' child (sometimes referred to as 'approved kinship carers').

> *Example*
>
> Emma is studying full time for an HND in social care. She is single and fosters a 13-year-old boy. She is eligible for IS.

Couples

If you have a child and your partner is also a full-time student, you are not excluded from IS in the summer vacation.[26] To be eligible, you must be in one of

Chapter 7: Income support
2. Who is eligible

the groups of people who can get IS (eg, a carer), listed under 'studying part time' on pbelow. Your child must be under 16, or under 20 and still a qualifying young person (see p9). During term time and short vacations, you are not eligible for IS.

If your partner is not a full-time student or is a part-time student, s/he is not excluded from IS and can get IS for you as well as for her/himself whether or not you have a child. S/he can get IS throughout the year, not just in the long vacation. To be eligible, s/he must be in one of the groups of people who can get IS listed below.

Refugees

Your English course must be more than 15 hours a week and aimed at helping you get work. You must have refugee status and you must have been in Britain for a year or less when your course starts. Payment of IS is limited to nine months.[27]

Under 22 without parental support

To qualify, you must be on a full-time course of non-advanced education on which you were accepted, enrolled or started before you turned 21.[28] If you turn 21 on your course, you continue to be eligible. In addition, you must:
- be an orphan, and no one is acting in place of your parent; *or*
- live away from your parents, or anyone acting in their place, because you are estranged from them; *or*
- live away from your parents because there is a serious risk or danger to you; *or*
- live away from your parents. They must be unable to support you financially and be sick or disabled, in prison or not allowed to enter Britain.

For more details, see the first four groups who are eligible for IS in relevant education listed on p53.

Under 19 in full-time advanced education

If you are under 19 and in full-time advanced education rather than in non-advanced education, the rules are the same as for those aged 19 or over. You count as a full-time student if you are 'attending or undertaking a full-time course of advanced education'.[29] What is or is not a full-time course is the same as for over-19-year-olds (see p55). Only some students can get IS. The groups who can get IS are the same as for full-time students aged 19 or over (see p55).

Studying part time

Part-time students can get IS under the usual rules without restriction. You must satisfy all the basic rules (see p60) and you must be in one of the groups of people who are eligible for IS. In brief, these are:
- lone parents under age 18 (regardless of the child's age) or lone parents with a child under five;

Chapter 7: Income support
2. Who is eligible

- some young people up to age 25 on youth training schemes;
- carers who get carer's allowance or care for someone who gets attendance allowance, the middle or highest rate of the disability living allowance care component, or the daily living component of personal independence payment;
- pregnant women from 11 weeks before to 15 weeks after the birth (or earlier if they are incapable of work because of pregnancy);
- single foster parents of children under 16 or with a child placed for adoption, or people looking after a child while their partner is abroad or if the parents are temporarily ill, or away temporarily;
- some people on unpaid paternity or parental leave;
- people caring for a family member who is temporarily ill;
- refugees on English courses in their first year in Britain;
- people entitled to statutory sick pay;
- people appealing against a decision that they are not incapable of work;
- people who are incapable of work, but only if they already get incapacity benefit (IB);[30]
- people who are registered or certified as blind, but only if they already get IB.

For more details of all the groups of people who are eligible for IS, see CPAG's *Welfare Benefits and Tax Credits Handbook*.

What counts as part time

You are regarded as a part-time student if you are not a full-time student. If you are under 20 and in relevant education, see p52 for who counts as full time. If you are in advanced education at any age or you are 19 or over and in non-advanced education (and not a 19-year-old in relevant education), see p55 for who counts as full time.

If you are at an FE college studying a non-advanced course such as NQ up to Advanced Higher level, SVQ up to level 3 or National Certificate, the DWP may ask you for a learning agreement to show that the course is part time – ie, no more than 16 classroom hours, or 21 classroom plus structured study hours. Your college can provide you with this.

Example
Betty is a carer for her disabled mother and has been getting IS on this basis for two years. She starts studying at college 12 hours a week towards a National Certificate. She continues to be eligible for IS.

3. Basic rules

As well as being a student who is eligible, to qualify for income support (IS) you must also satisfy all the following conditions.[31]
- You are aged 16 or over.
- You have not reached pension age. If you have reached this age, you may be eligible for pension credit (PC) instead. Pension age is rising from 65 and is due to reach 66 by October 2020. See CPAG's *Welfare Benefits and Tax Credits Handbook* for more details.
- You are not working 16 hours or more a week. If you are working 16 hours or more, you may be eligible for working tax credit instead (see p109).
- Your partner is not working 24 hours or more a week.
- You are present in Great Britain, satisfy the 'habitual residence' and 'right to reside' tests, and are not a 'person subject to immigration control'. (You can sometimes be paid IS for the first four or eight weeks you are outside Britain.) These terms are explained in CPAG's *Welfare Benefits and Tax Credits Handbook*. Further advice is available from UKCISA (see Appendix 2).
- You have no more than £16,000 capital.
- Your income is less than the set amount the law says you need to live on (known as your 'applicable amount' – see p61).

4. Amount of benefit

The amount of income support (IS) you get depends on your and your partner's circumstances. The amount also depends on your income and capital. Go through the following steps to work out the amount of IS to which you are entitled.

Step one: capital

If your capital is over £16,000, you cannot get IS (see p157). Some kinds of capital are ignored. For details, see CPAG's *Welfare Benefits and Tax Credits Handbook*.

Step two: work out your applicable amount

This is an amount for basic weekly needs. It is made up of:
- personal allowances (see p62);
- premiums (see p63);
- housing costs (see p64).

Step three: work out your weekly income

Chapter 17 explains how your loan, grant or other income is taken into account and how to work out your weekly income.

Step four: deduct weekly income from applicable amount

If your income is *less* than your applicable amount, IS equals the difference between the two.

If your income is *the same as or more than* your applicable amount, you cannot get IS. You may be able to claim again (see p51) if your income goes down – eg, during the long vacation.

Example
Nora is 23 and a full-time, second-year undergraduate student and a lone parent of Penny, aged two. She gets a student loan of £6,750, plus an independent students' bursary of £1,000, £1,305 lone parents' grant and £1,215 for childcare. Her only other income is child benefit of £20.70 a week, child tax credit (CTC) of £63.63 a week, and personal independence payment (PIP) of £58.70 a week.

During the academic year September 2019 to June 2020:

Step one	Nora has no savings or capital.
Step two	Her applicable amount is:

Personal allowance for herself	£73.10
Disability premium	£34.35
Severe disability premium	£65.85
Total applicable amount	£173.30

Step three — Her weekly income is:

Loan	£168.02

The childcare grant and lone parents' grant are disregarded. Her loan (less certain disregards) is divided over the 42 weeks of the academic year (see Chapter 17). Child benefit, CTC and PIP are disregarded.

Step four — Her income is £5.28 below her applicable amount, so she can get IS of £5.28 a week from September 2019 to June 2020.

During the long vacation from June 2020 to September 2020:

Step two — At 2019/20 rates, Nora's applicable amount is £173.30 (as above).

Step three — Her weekly income for IS purposes from the end of June 2020 to the beginning of September 2020 is nil. This is because her loan only counts as income during the academic year. Child benefit, CTC and PIP are disregarded.

Step four — From the end of June 2020 to the beginning of September 2020 her weekly IS is £173.30. Nora's IS should increase from the end of June.

Applicable amount

Work out your applicable amount by adding together your personal allowances, premiums and eligible housing costs. Benefit rates are uprated in April each year.[32] It is usually possible to find out the new rates from the beginning of December.

Chapter 7: Income support
4. Amount of benefit

Check the DWP website at www.gov.uk/government/organisations/department-for-work-pensions for a press release on social security uprating. The amounts in this *Handbook* are from April 2019.

Personal allowance

Your personal allowance is made up of the following.[33]
- One personal allowance at either the single, lone parent or couple rate depending on your situation. The amount depends on your age.

Circumstances	£ per week	Conditions
Single		
Under 25	57.90	No special conditions.
25 or over	73.10	No special conditions.
Lone parent		
Under 18	57.90	No special conditions.
18 or over	73.10	No special conditions.
Couple		
Both aged 16–17 (certain cases)	87.50	You get this rate if: – you or your partner are responsible for a child; *or* – you and your partner would be eligible for IS or income-related employment and support allowance (ESA) if you were single; *or* – your partner is eligible for income-based jobseeker's allowance (JSA) or severe hardship payments of JSA.
Both aged 16–17 (everyone else)	57.90	For everyone else who cannot get the higher rate.
One aged 16–17, one 18 or over	114.85	The younger partner: – is eligible for IS or income-related ESA, or would be if s/he were single; *or* – is eligible for income-based JSA; *or* – is entitled to severe hardship payments of JSA.
One aged 16–17, one 18–24	57.90	For those who are not eligible for the rate above.
One aged 16–17, one 25 or over	73.10	For those who are not eligible for the rate above.
Both aged 18 or over	114.85	No special conditions.

Chapter 7: Income support
4. Amount of benefit

Premiums

Qualifying for premiums depends on your circumstances.
You can qualify for either one, but not both, of the following.
- **Disability premium** of £34.35 (£48.95 for a couple). You get a disability premium if you get:[34]
  - disability living allowance (DLA);
  - PIP;
  - long-term incapacity benefit (IB);
  - severe disablement allowance;
  - working tax credit with a disabled worker or severe disability element;
  - war pensioner's mobility supplement;
  - constant attendance allowance;
  - exceptionally severe disablement allowance.

  You also qualify if:
  - you are certified as severely sight impaired or blind, and for 28 weeks after coming off the register; *or*
  - you are terminally ill and have been entitled to statutory sick pay (SSP) for at least 196 days; *or*
  - you have been receiving a disability premium since before October 2008 because of incapacity for work.

  If you are the IS claimant and you have a partner, you get the disability premium if s/he gets any of the qualifying benefits or is blind.
- **Pensioner premium** of £140.40 for couples. People who have reached pension age claim pension credit (PC) (see p60) claim PC rather than IS. However, you get a pensioner premium if you are under this age and getting IS and you have a partner who has reached this age.[35]

In addition, you can qualify for any, or all, of the following.[36]
- **Carer premium** of £36.85. You get a carer premium if you are entitled to carer's allowance (CA) (see p4). If you are entitled to CA but not paid it because it overlaps with another benefit (eg, IB), you still qualify for a carer premium. You get two carer premiums if both you and your partner qualify.
- **Enhanced disability premium** for an adult of £16.84 (£24.10 for a couple). You get this premium if you get the highest rate of the DLA care component or the enhanced rate of the PIP daily living component.[37]
- **Severe disability premium** of £65.85. This is a premium for severely disabled people who live alone, or can be treated as living alone. You qualify for this premium if you get the middle or highest rate of the DLA care component, or the standard or enhanced rate of the PIP daily living component, and no one gets CA for looking after you. You do not get it if you live with another person aged 18 or over (eg, a friend or parent), unless s/he is separately liable for rent, or you only share a bathroom or hallway, or in some other circumstances.[38]
See CPAG's *Welfare Benefits and Tax Credits Handbook* for details. If you have a

Chapter 7: Income support
5. Claiming income support

partner, you do not qualify unless s/he also qualifies in her/his own right or is severely sight impaired or blind. If you both qualify, you get two premiums.

Housing costs

IS can include amounts for certain service charges if you own your home.

If you own your own home and get IS, you may be able to get a loan from the DWP to help with the cost of your mortgage interest payments,[39] repayable when you sell your home or on your death. Payments are usually made directly to your mortgage lender. Usually help only starts once you have been getting IS for 39 weeks, although there are some exceptions to this. **Note:** these loans are not part of your IS.

Normally you have to live in the home you own to get a loan for mortgage interest, but there are exceptions for full-time students (and some others). You can still get a loan for mortgage interest if you have moved elsewhere to study but are not paying rent or mortgage at the term-time address. If you pay for both places, you can get a loan for both if you are a couple and it is unavoidable that you live in two separate homes. Otherwise, you can get a loan if you are away from your home temporarily and have not let it out and are not likely to be away for more than 52 weeks.[40]

You must claim universal credit (see Chapter 11), or, in some cases, housing benefit (see Chapter 6) for help with your rent.

For more details, see CPAG's *Welfare Benefits and Tax Credits Handbook*.

5. Claiming income support

If you can still claim income support (IS) (see p51), claim as soon as you can. There are only very limited situations in which backdating is allowed.

To start your claim, contact Jobcentre Plus on 0800 169 0350 (textphone 0800 023 4888).

When you call, details of your claim are taken and a date for a work-focused interview is arranged (unless it is agreed that you do not need to attend one). A call-back can be arranged if a single call is not appropriate – eg, if you have language or hearing difficulties. You are sent a statement to check and sign, and you are told what evidence and information you should take to your interview or forward to the DWP. The work-focused interview is intended to help you into full-time work, even if you have no intention of working until you finish your studies, but you are under no obligation to look for work.

If you cannot, or do not want to, use the telephone to start your claim, you should still be able to claim in other ways. A claim form should still be accepted, which you can get from Jobcentre Plus, or you may be able to start a claim online at www.gov.uk. It is important to let your Jobcentre Plus office know you want to claim IS, as otherwise you might lose benefit. You should return the form within one month of your initial contact.

Either member of a couple can make the claim for both, but whoever claims must be eligible in her/his own right.

Getting paid

Payment is usually made directly into your bank or building society. Which account it goes into is up to you. If you do not want your benefit to go into an account that is already overdrawn, give the DWP details of an alternative account if you have access to, or can open, one. If you do not have an account, you are usually expected to open one with a bank, building society or post office.

If your claim is refused

Your claim may be unsuccessful for a variety of reasons, including if your student income is too high to qualify. However, you might find that you qualify in the long vacation because of the way your grant and loan are divided up through the year. So if you are turned down, claim again as soon as you think you might qualify (provided you are eligible to make a new claim – see p51).

6. Challenging a decision

If you think a decision about your income support is wrong, you can ask the DWP to look at it again. This process is known as a 'mandatory reconsideration'. Provided you ask within the time limit (usually one month), the DWP notifies you of the decision in a 'mandatory reconsideration notice'. If you are still not happy when you get this notice, you can appeal to the independent First-tier Tribunal. If it was not possible to ask the DWP to reconsider the decision within a month, you can ask for a late revision (within 13 months), explaining why it is late. You can also ask the DWP to look at a decision again at any time if certain grounds are met – eg, if there has been an official error.

7. Other benefits and tax credits

Income support (IS) tops up other income you have to the level of your basic requirements (your 'applicable amount'). Most other benefits you get are therefore taken into account as income when working out your IS. This means they reduce your IS pound for pound. Disability living allowance, personal independence payment and housing benefit (HB) are, however, always disregarded as income.

If you have children and get child tax credit (CTC), both CTC and child benefit are disregarded as income for IS.

Chapter 7: Income support
Notes

Getting another benefit may reduce your IS, but might also mean you qualify for a premium with your IS (eg, getting carer's allowance means you qualify for a carer premium), so you could be better off overall (although in this case, the person you care for could get less benefit – see p6).

If you get IS and you pay rent, you are eligible as a student for HB (unless you are a care leaver aged 16 or 17).

IS is taken into account when calculating whether the benefit cap applies (see p49 and p98).

Passported benefits

Provided you meet any other conditions, getting IS entitles you to:
- free dental treatment;
- vouchers for glasses;
- a Best Start grant;
- Best Start foods;
- funeral support payments;
- a budgeting loan;
- free school lunches from your local authority.

See Chapters 5 and 14 for details.

Notes

2. Who is eligible
1. s124(1)(d) SSCBA 1992
2. Reg 12 IS Regs; s142 SSCBA 1992
3. Reg 1(3) CB Regs
4. Reg 13(2) and Sch 1B para 15 IS Regs
5. DWP guidance, 'Making a Severe Hardship Decision', paras 7 and 28, available at www.gov.uk. This guidance is for JSA but should equally apply for IS.
6. Vol 4, para 20686 DMG
7. CIS/4096/2005
8. Vol 4, para 20693 DMG
9. Reg 2 C(LC)SSB(S) Regs
10. Reg 14(2) IS Regs; reg 76(2) JSA Regs
11. Reg 3(2)(b) CB Regs
12. Reg 4 CB Regs
13. Reg 13(2A)(b) IS Regs; reg 5 CB Regs
14. Reg 7 CB Regs
15. Reg 4ZA(2) IS Regs
16. Regs 2(1), definition of 'period of study', and 61(1), definition of 'last day of the course', IS Regs
17. Reg 61(2)(b) IS Regs
18. Reg 61(1), definition of 'full-time student', IS Regs
19. R(SB) 40/83; R(SB) 41/83
20. Reg 61(1)(c), definition of 'full-time course of study', IS Regs
21. Reg 61(1), definition of 'sandwich course', IS Regs; reg 4(2) The Education (Student Loans) (Scotland) Regulations 2007, No.154
22. Reg 61(4) IS Regs
23. Vol 6, para 30238 DMG
24. Reg 4ZA(3) IS Regs
25. Sch 1B para 1 IS Regs; s137 SSCBA 1992

Chapter 7: Income support
Notes

26 Reg 4ZA(3)(c) IS Regs
27 Sch 1B para 18 IS Regs
28 Sch 1B para 15A IS Regs
29 Reg 61(1), definition of 'full-time student', IS Regs
30 Regs 1(4) and 2(1) ESA(TP) Regs

3. Basic rules
31 s124 SSCBA 1992

4. Amount of benefit
32 s11 WRWA 2016
33 Sch 2 para 1 IS Regs
34 Sch 2 paras 11 and 12 IS Regs
35 Sch 2 paras 9, 9A and 10 IS Regs
36 Sch 2 para 6 IS Regs
37 Sch 2 paras 13A and 15(8) IS Regs
38 Sch 2 para 13 IS Regs
39 Reg 3 LMI Regs
40 Sch 3 para 4 LMI Regs

Chapter 8

Jobseeker's allowance

This chapter covers:
1. What is jobseeker's allowance (below)
2. Who is eligible (p69)
3. Basic rules (p74)
4. Amount of benefit (p75)
5. Claiming jobseeker's allowance (p77)
6. Challenging a decision (p77)
7. Other benefits and tax credits (p78)

> **Basic facts**
> – Jobseeker's allowance provides basic financial support for people who are expected to 'sign on' for work.
> – Full-time students are not normally eligible.
> – Student couples with children and lone parents may be eligible in the long vacation.
> – Part-time students are eligible if they are available for work.
> – You do not need to have paid national insurance contributions to qualify, but you might get more money if you have.
> – The amount is usually affected by any grant, loan or other income you may have.

1. What is jobseeker's allowance

Jobseeker's allowance (JSA) provides basic financial support for people of working age who are not working full time and who are expected to 'sign on' as available for work.

Full-time students are normally excluded from JSA, but there are exceptions. Part-time students are eligible if they are available for work.

If you have paid sufficient national insurance contributions, you get contribution-based JSA for the first six months. This is paid on top of any student or other income you might have. Otherwise, you may get income-based JSA. This is means tested, so most of your student income and most other income is taken

Chapter 8: Jobseeker's allowance
2. Who is eligible

into account when working out how much benefit you get. Chapter 17 explains how your income affects your benefit.

Note: you cannot usually make a new claim for income-based JSA, as it is in the process of being replaced by universal credit. However, an exception applies if you get, or got in the past month (and continue to satisfy the rules for it), a severe disability premium in your income-based JSA, income support, income-related employment and support allowance or housing benefit.

2. Who is eligible

As new claims cannot usually be made for income-based jobseeker's allowance (JSA) (see p68 for exceptions), most students getting income-based JSA will be those who were already on this before starting the course, and who are eligible for income-based JSA as a student (which mainly applies to part-time students). If you cannot claim income-based JSA, you may be able to get universal credit instead (see Chapter 11).

To qualify for JSA, you must not be excluded as a student, and you must satisfy the basic rules. See below for details of students who are eligible. The basic rules are covered on p74.

Note: the following rules for full-time students and young people in relevant education do *not* apply to contribution-based JSA if you are making a new claim for JSA and you do not already get income support (IS), income-related employment and support allowance (ESA) or housing benefit (HB) that includes a severe disability premium. This is sometimes called 'new-style' JSA. You can only get 'new-style' contribution-based JSA and study full time if you took time out of your course because of illness or caring responsibilities, you have now recovered or the caring responsibilities have ended, and you are waiting to rejoin your course.[1]

Under 20 in relevant education

You cannot get JSA while in 'relevant education'.[2]

Relevant education
You are in **'relevant education'** if:
– your course is non-advanced (ie, school level or below degree, Higher National Certificate or Higher National Diploma level) of more than 12 hours a week;[3] *and*
– you are under 19, or aged 19 and were accepted on, enrolled on or started your course before you turned 19.

This is the same definition as that used for child benefit and similar to that for child tax credit (CTC). So, although you cannot get JSA for yourself, your parents may still be able to get child benefit and CTC for you.

A special rule allows part-time students who have been on benefit for some months to study and get JSA at the same time, even though their course is over 12 hours a week. This applies if your course is not full time according to the rules below that apply to most students over 19, and you got JSA or ESA, or you were on an Employability Fund course or other similar training:
- during the last three months before the start of the course; *or*
- for three out of the last six months before the course if you were working the rest of the time.

19 or over and a full-time student

You cannot usually get JSA as a full-time student aged 19 or over (and not in relevant education – see p69), whether in advanced or non-advanced education, at any time during your 'period of study'.[4]

Period of study

Your **'period of study'** is the whole of your course from the first day you attend or undertake the course to the last day – ie, the last day of the final academic year, including short and long vacations.[5] It includes a period of study in connection with the course after you have stopped doing the course itself. It does not include freshers' week, unless your course actually starts that week.[6]

You are not a student in between courses. For example, you can get JSA in the summer between completing an undergraduate degree and starting a postgraduate course.

Postgraduates writing up their thesis at the end of a course may be regarded by the DWP as being in 'a period of study undertaken by the student in connection with the course'. However, guidance for decision makers says someone is 'not a full-time student during the period after the end of the course when they are expected to complete any course work'.[7] To get JSA, you must show that you are available for and actively looking for work. If you say you are not prepared to fit your thesis writing around a job, should one come up, the DWP will decide that you are not available for work.

What counts as full time

In most cases, the college or university defines whether the course is full or part time. However, for some further education (FE) students, there is a 16/21-hour study rule. The JSA rules are the same as those for IS (see p55).

Chapter 8: Jobseeker's allowance
2. Who is eligible

Who can get jobseeker's allowance

You can get JSA in the following circumstances. **Note:** you cannot usually make a new claim for income-based JSA (see p68).

- You are in a couple, both of you are full-time students and you have a dependent child aged under 16, or aged under 20 and a qualifying young person (see p9). You can get JSA during the summer vacation only. The person who claims must be available for work and meet all the other basic rules for JSA.[8]
- You are a single person with a dependent child aged under 16, or aged under 20 and a qualifying young person (see p9). You can get JSA during the summer vacation only. You must be available for work and meet all the other basic rules for JSA.[9]
- Your course must be regarded by your work coach at the Jobcentre Plus office as a qualifying course. You must be aged 25 or over and have been getting JSA for at least two years before the course starts. During term time you are not expected to sign on or look for work, although you may be required to provide evidence of your attendance and progress on the course. During vacations, you are expected to look for casual work.[10]
- You are on a full-time employment-related course approved by your work coach at the Jobcentre Plus office. You can get JSA for just two weeks.[11]

Under 19 and in full-time advanced education

You cannot usually get JSA if you are under 19 and studying full time in advanced education. The rules are the same for you as they are for full-time students aged 19 or over (see p70).

Studying part time

You can get JSA while studying part time. You must continue to pass all the basic rules for JSA, including being available for work and actively looking for work.

What counts as part time

Generally, your college or university determines whether you count as a part-time or full-time student, rather than the number of hours you study or attend lectures.[12] The rules are the same as for IS (see p59).

However, if you are under age 20 and in relevant education, there is a 12-hour rule (see p52). Your course is full time if it is more than 12 hours a week of classes and supervised study in term time.

If you are aged 19 or over (and not a 19-year-old in 'relevant education') at an FE college but not on a higher education course, there is a 16/21-hour rule for courses funded, or partly funded, by the Scottish government. A part-time course is:[13]

- up to 16 hours a week classroom or workshop-guided learning, under the direct guidance of teaching staff; *or*
- up to 21 hours when hours of structured learning are added on, provided classes are no more than 16 hours a week.

This is set out in a learning agreement provided by your college.

Examples
Shona is 20 and attending an FE college, studying for National Qualifications at higher level. She has 10 hours a week of classes and 10 hours a week of timetabled independent study. She is classed as a part-time student.

Gwyneth is 24 and at an FE college on a Scottish Vocational Qualification level 2 course. She has classes for 18 hours a week and three hours of timetabled study. She is classed as a full-time student.

Russell is 18 and studying for a National Certificate. He has 15 hours of classes a week. He is classed as full time.

Saleem is 19 and studying for a degree. He has 15 hours of lectures a week. The university regards his course as full time. He is classed as a full-time student for JSA.

Studying and availability for work

If you are getting JSA, you may have agreed which hours of the day and which days of the week you are available for work. This 'pattern of availability' is set out in your 'claimant commitment'. You are allowed to do this provided the hours you choose still give you a reasonable chance of getting work and do not considerably reduce your prospects of getting work.

If the hours you study are completely different to the hours you have agreed to be available for work, you should have no problem. If, however, there is some overlap, or if you have agreed to be available for work at any time of day and on any day of the week, the DWP must be satisfied that you are available for work despite your course. It expects you to:
- rearrange the hours of your course to fit round a job or be prepared to give up the course if a job comes up; *and*
- be ready to take time off the course to attend a job interview; *and*
- be ready to start work immediately.

Guidance tells DWP decision makers to look at various factors when deciding whether you are genuinely available for work, such as:[14]
- what you are doing to look for work;
- whether your course will help you get work. Bear in mind that if you say the course is necessary to get the kind of job you want, the DWP may assume you

are not prepared to give it up to do another kind of job and, therefore, decide you are not available for work;
- whether you can be contacted about a possible job if you are studying away from home;
- whether you gave up work or training to do the course;
- your hours of attendance on the course;
- whether it is possible to change the hours if necessary;
- whether you could still complete the course if you missed some classes;
- how much you paid for the course and whether any fees could be refunded if you gave up the course. The DWP is likely to assume that you are not prepared to give up the course to take a job if you have paid a significant amount in course fees;
- whether any grant would need to be repaid if you gave up your course.

At the Jobcentre Plus office you are given a student questionnaire, Form ES567S *Attending a Training or Education Course*, to complete.

However, the DWP does not need to know about any of the above factors if you got JSA, incapacity benefit, IS on incapacity for work grounds or ESA, or were on an Employability Fund course or similar training:
- during the last three months before the start of the course; *or*
- for three out of the last six months before the course if you were working the rest of the time.

If this applies to you and your course hours overlap with your pattern of availability but you are willing and able to rearrange them in order to take up employment, no other questions about your course are relevant to your availability for work.[15] You need only complete Part 1 of the student questionnaire and sign Part 3.

Once you have qualified for JSA, you must continue to be available for work and actively look for work. When you 'sign on', you must show what steps you have taken to look for work – eg, checked job adverts or applied for jobs. If you do not look for work each week, or you turn down a job or interview, you could be given a sanction and lose some or all of your JSA, which could be for up to three years. If this happens, you can appeal. You might be able to reduce the amount of the sanction or have it overturned. Get advice about this and ask for a hardship payment in the meantime.

Open University students can attend a residential course for up to a week and keep their JSA. You are not expected to be available for, or to look for, work during that week.[16]

16/17-year-olds

Usually you can only get JSA if you are aged 18 or over. If you are under 18, you can get income-based JSA in the following circumstances, provided you meet all the other entitlement conditions.

Chapter 8: Jobseeker's allowance
3. Basic rules

- You are in severe hardship. All your circumstances should be considered. Payments are discretionary and usually for just eight weeks at a time.
- You come within one of the groups of people who can claim IS. These are the same groups as for part-time students who can claim IS (see p58).
- You are a couple with a child.
- You are married or in a civil partnership and your partner is aged 18 or over. JSA is paid for a limited period after you leave full-time education.
- You are married or in a civil partnership and your partner is under 18 and registered for work or training, or long-term sick or disabled, or a student who can claim IS, or a carer who can claim IS. JSA is paid for a limited period after you leave full-time education.
- You are leaving local authority care and are a lone parent.[17] JSA is usually paid for just eight weeks. **Note:** your local authority social work department may give financial support if you have been in care.

3. Basic rules

As well as being a student who is eligible for jobseeker's allowance (JSA), you must satisfy all of the basic rules.[18]

- You are available for work. You must be willing and able to take up work immediately (although some people are allowed notice). You must be prepared to work at least 40 hours a week. People with caring responsibilities and disabled people can restrict themselves to fewer than 40 hours. During your child's school holidays, you are not expected to be available for work if there is no childcare reasonable for you to arrange, but this provision does not apply if you are a full-time student.[19]
- You are actively seeking work.
- You have a claimant commitment. This sets out, for instance, the hours you have agreed to work, the type of work you are looking for and any restrictions on travel and pay.
- If you are doing any work, it is for less than 16 hours a week. You can get contribution-based JSA if your partner is working, but not income-based JSA unless s/he works less than 24 hours a week.
- You are capable of work (although you can continue to get JSA for up to 13 weeks while sick).
- You are under pension age (rising from age 65, and will be 66 by October 2020).
- You are in Great Britain, although JSA can be paid in other countries in some circumstances. See CPAG's *Welfare Benefits and Tax Credits Handbook* for details.
- You meet the conditions for either contribution-based JSA or income-based JSA (see p75). If you meet the conditions for both, you get contribution-based JSA topped up by income-based JSA.

Contribution-based jobseeker's allowance

You must have paid sufficient national insurance contributions to qualify for contribution-based JSA, as well as meeting all the basic rules on p74.[20]

You must have paid class 1 contributions on earnings of at least the lower earnings limit in 26 weeks, which need not be consecutive, in one of the two complete tax years (6 April to 5 April) before the start of the benefit year (which runs from the first Sunday in January) in which you claim. You also must have paid or been credited with class 1 contributions on earnings of 50 times the lower earnings limit in these years.

For example, you qualify if you claim JSA in 2019 and you paid contributions on earnings of £5,600 in the tax year April 2016 to April 2017 and £5,650 in the tax year April 2017 to April 2018, earning in the first year £112 a week or more, or in the second year £113 a week or more, for at least 26 weeks.

Income-based jobseeker's allowance

As well as satisfying all the basic rules above, to get income-based JSA you must meet the following conditions.[21]
- You are aged 18 or over. You can still get income-based JSA if you are aged 16 or 17 but there are extra rules (see p73).
- You satisfy the 'habitual residence' and 'right to reside' tests, and are not a 'person subject to immigration control'. These terms are explained in CPAG's *Welfare Benefits and Tax Credits Handbook*. Further advice for overseas students is available from UKCISA (see Appendix 2).
- Your income is below the amount set for your basic living needs (known as your 'applicable amount').
- You have no more than £16,000 capital. See Chapter 17 for how your income and capital affect your benefits.
- You do not get pension credit.

4. Amount of benefit

Jobseeker's allowance (JSA) is payable after seven 'waiting days'. You may get contribution-based JSA and/or income-based JSA, depending on your circumstances.

Contribution-based jobseeker's allowance

The amount of contribution-based JSA depends on your age.

Chapter 8: Jobseeker's allowance
4. Amount of benefit

Weekly rate from April 2019
Under 25   £57.90
25 or over   £73.10

You may get less than this if you have part-time earnings or an occupational or personal pension, but the amount is not affected by a student loan or grant. Contribution-based JSA is only paid for up to 26 weeks. After that, you can claim income-based JSA if your income is low enough. Unlike income-based JSA, you only get amounts for yourself, not for a partner.

Income-based jobseeker's allowance

Income-based JSA is worked out in the same way as income support (IS). The amount you get is made up of:
- personal allowances;
- premiums;
- housing costs – ie, certain service charges.

The total of these is called your 'applicable amount'. If you have no other income (the student loan and some grants count as income), you are paid your full applicable amount. Otherwise, any income you have is topped up with income-based JSA to the level of your applicable amount. If your weekly income is above your applicable amount, you are not entitled to income-based JSA. See Chapter 17 for how to work out your weekly income. See Chapter 7 for how to work out your applicable amount. The rules are almost the same as for IS, with the following differences.
- If you are in a couple and only one of you is under 18, you get the higher £114.85 personal allowance if the younger partner is responsible for a child or is eligible for income-based JSA, severe hardship payments, IS (or would be if not a member of a couple) or income-related employment and support allowance (ESA).
- If you are in a couple and both of you are under 18, you get the higher £87.50 personal allowance if:
  – you or your partner are responsible for a child;
  – both of you would be eligible for income-based JSA, or your partner would be eligible for IS or income-related ESA if you were both single;
  – you are both eligible for severe hardship payments, or one of you is while the other is eligible for income-based JSA, IS or income-related ESA;
  – you are married or civil partners and one of you is registered with Skills Development Scotland, or both of you are eligible for income-based JSA.
- If you are in a 'joint-claim couple' (see p77), you can get a disability premium (at the couple rate) if one of you has had limited capability for work for 364

days (196 days if terminally ill). You must claim ESA to establish limited capability for work, even if you might not get it.

5. Claiming jobseeker's allowance

You start your claim for contribution-based jobseeker's allowance (JSA) online (see www.gov.uk/jobseekers-allowance/how-to-claim). If you are claiming JSA, rather than universal credit, because you qualify for a severe disability premium in another benefit (eg, housing benefit or employment and support allowance) (see p68), you start your claim by phoning Jobcentre Plus on 0800 055 6688 (textphone 0800 023 4888).

You are given an appointment for an interview. Claim as soon as you can, as JSA can only be backdated in very limited circumstances. If you are under 18, you should register with Skills Development Scotland first.

At the interview, you are asked to complete Form ES2, *Helping You Back to Work*, which has questions about looking for work. When filling in this form, remember that even though you are a student, you are expected to be available for work and actively looking for work. Make sure your answers do not cast doubt on your willingness to work. If you are a part-time student, you are also given the student questionnaire to complete and are asked for a learning agreement from your college to show that you are studying part time.

Couples

If you are a full-time student or in relevant education but your partner is not, s/he can get JSA for both of you if s/he is eligible for JSA.[22] You both need to claim, but only your partner must continue to sign on and look for work. Similarly, your partner can get JSA for both of you if you are not yet a full-time student, but you have applied for, or been accepted on, a course.

Most other couples, including if one or both of you are part-time students, need to claim income-based JSA jointly. This means that both of you must make the claim, be eligible for JSA, sign on and look for work.

Some people need not claim jointly. Only the person who makes the claim for the couple must be eligible and sign on if:
- you have dependent children; *or*
- you are both under 18.

6. Challenging a decision

If you think a decision about your jobseeker's allowance is wrong, you can ask the DWP to look at it again. This process is known as a 'mandatory reconsideration'.

Provided you ask within the time limit (usually one month), the DWP notifies you of the decision in a 'mandatory reconsideration notice'. If you are still not happy when you get this notice, you can appeal to the independent First-tier Tribunal. If it was not possible to ask the DWP to reconsider the decision within a month, you can ask for a late revision (within 13 months), explaining why it is late. You can also ask the DWP to look at a decision again at any time if certain grounds are met – eg, if there has been an official error.

7. **Other benefits and tax credits**

If you get contribution-based jobseeker's allowance (JSA), you can claim universal credit as well. You cannot get income support (IS) and JSA at the same time, so if you are eligible for both, you must choose which to claim. In general, the amounts of income-based JSA and IS are the same, but you are not expected to sign on for work for IS.

Child tax credit (CTC) and, except for some existing claimants, child benefit are ignored as income when JSA is assessed. If you have been getting income-based JSA since before 6 April 2004 and still have amounts for children included in your JSA, child benefit is taken into account as income.

If you get income-based JSA, you are also eligible as a student for housing benefit provided you meet the other rules of entitlement.

JSA is taken into account when calculating whether the benefit cap applies (see p49 and p98).

Passported benefits

Provided you meet any other conditions, getting income-based JSA entitles you to:
- free dental treatment;
- vouchers for glasses;
- a Best Start grant;
- Best Start foods;
- funeral support payments;
- a budgeting loan;
- free school lunches from the local authority.

Contribution-based JSA does not give you automatic access to these benefits, but you may qualify for health benefits on low income grounds. See Chapter 5 for details.

Chapter 8: Jobseeker's allowance
Notes

Notes

2. Who is eligible
1. Reg 45(6) JSA Regs 2013
2. s1(2)(g) JSA 1995
3. Reg 54 JSA Regs
4. Reg 15(1)(a) JSA Regs
5. Regs 4 and 130 JSA Regs
6. Vol 6, para 30221 DMG
7. Vol 6, para 30238 DMG
8. Reg 15(2) and (3) JSA Regs
9. Reg 15(2) and (3) JSA Regs
10. Regs 17A and 21A JSA Regs
11. Reg 14(1)(a) JSA Regs
12. Reg 1(b)(i), definition of 'full-time student', JSA Regs
13. Reg 1(b)(iii), definition of 'full-time student', JSA Regs
14. Vol 4, para 21242 DMG
15. Reg 11 JSA Regs
16. Regs 14(1)(f) and 19(1)(f) JSA Regs
17. C(LC)SSB(S) Regs

3. Basic rules
18. s1 JSA 1995
19. Reg 15(4) JSA Regs
20. s2 JSA 1995
21. ss3 and 13 JSA 1995

5. Claiming jobseeker's allowance
22. Sch A1 JSA Regs; Vol 6, para 30245 DMG

Chapter 9
Maternity, paternity and adoption benefits

This chapter covers:
1. What are maternity, paternity and adoption benefits (below)
2. Who is eligible (p81)
3. Amount of benefit (p83)
4. Claiming maternity, paternity and adoption benefits (p83)
5. Challenging a decision (p83)
6. Other benefits and tax credits (p84)

> **Basic facts**
> – Women having a baby can claim statutory maternity pay if they have an employer, or maternity allowance if they have recently worked.
> – The mother's partner can claim statutory paternity pay.
> – Parents adopting a child can claim statutory adoption pay (SAP) and statutory paternity pay (SPP) – one partner can claim SAP and the other SPP.
> – Either partner in a couple can claim statutory shared parental pay instead of statutory maternity, paternity or adoption pay.
> – Part-time and full-time students are eligible for these benefits.

1. What are maternity, paternity and adoption benefits

Statutory maternity pay

You can get statutory maternity pay (SMP) for 39 weeks if you are pregnant or have just had a baby, have an employer and earn at least £118 a week (April 2019 rate).

Maternity allowance

If you cannot get SMP but you have recently worked, either employed or self-employed, you may be able to get maternity allowance (MA) for 39 weeks. You may also qualify if you have helped your partner with her/his self-employment. See CPAG's *Welfare Benefits and Tax Credits Handbook* for details.

Statutory paternity pay

You can get statutory paternity pay (SPP) for two weeks if your partner is having a baby and you are taking leave from work to care for her or for the child. You can also get statutory shared parental pay (SSPP) in some circumstances. See CPAG's *Welfare Benefits and Tax Credits Handbook* for details. Unmarried partners, including same-sex partners, can claim SPP.

Statutory adoption pay

You can get statutory adoption pay (SAP) for 39 weeks if you are adopting a child and are earning at least £118 a week from employment (April 2019 rate). If a couple (including same-sex couples) are adopting a child, one can claim SAP and the other can claim SPP for two weeks (or SSPP, in some circumstances).

Statutory shared parental pay

You or your partner can get SSPP instead of SMP, MA or SAP in certain circumstances.

2. Who is eligible

Students are eligible for maternity, paternity and adoption benefits if they pass the basic rules for these. See CPAG's *Welfare Benefits and Tax Credits Handbook* for details. What follows is a brief outline of the qualifying conditions.

Statutory maternity pay

You can get statutory maternity pay (SMP) if:
- you are pregnant or have recently had a baby;
- you have worked for the same employer for 26 weeks ending with the 15th week before your expected week of birth;
- your average gross earnings are at least £118 a week (April 2019 rate); *and*
- you give your employer the correct notice.

Maternity allowance

You can get maternity allowance (MA) if you cannot get SMP and:
- you are pregnant or have recently had a baby;

- you have worked, either as an employee or self-employed, for at least 26 weeks out of the 66 weeks before the expected week of birth; *and*
- your average earnings are at least £30 a week.

Statutory paternity pay

You can get statutory paternity pay (SPP) if:
- you are the child's father or partner of the child's mother and you will be caring for the child or supporting the mother;
- you have worked for the same employer for 41 weeks before the baby is born;
- your average gross earnings are at least £118 a week (April 2019 rate); *and*
- you give your employer the correct notice.

You can also get SPP if you are adopting a child – you cannot get SPP for adoption and statutory adoption pay (SAP) at the same time, although one member of a couple can claim SAP while the other claims SPP (for adoption).

Statutory adoption pay

You can get SAP if:
- you are adopting a child;
- you have worked for the same employer for 26 weeks ending with the week in which you are told you have been matched with a child for adoption;
- your average gross earnings are at least £118 a week (April 2019 rate); *and*
- you give your employer the correct notice.

Statutory shared parental pay

You can get SSPP if you are caring for a child and either:
- you are the mother of the child or have adopted the child, and you have reduced your MA, SMP or SAP period; *or*
- you are the father of the child or the partner of the mother/adopter and your partner has reduced her/his MA, SMP or SAP period.

Your partner must also meet employment and earnings tests. See CPAG's *Welfare Benefits and Tax Credits Handbook* for more details.

3. Amount of benefit

Weekly rate from April 2019

Statutory maternity pay (SMP)	for the first six weeks	90% of average weekly earnings
	for the following 33 weeks	£148.68 (or 90% of earnings if less)
Statutory paternity pay (SPP)	for two weeks	£148.68 (or 90% of earnings if less)
Statutory adoption pay (SAP)	for 39 weeks	£148.68 (or 90% of earnings if less)
Statutory shared parental pay (SSPP)	for 37 weeks	£148.68 (or 90% of earnings if less)
Maternity allowance (MA)	for 39 weeks	£148.68 (or 90% of earnings if less)

You can end your SMP, SAP or MA early and your partner can take parental leave instead of you and be paid SSPP. Or you can end your SMP, SAP or MA early and get SSPP yourself, as it gives you more flexibility in when you take your paid leave. See CPAG's *Welfare Benefits and Tax Credits Handbook* for more details.

4. Claiming maternity, paternity and adoption benefits

You claim statutory maternity, adoption, paternity and shared parental pay from your employer. You claim maternity allowance from your local Jobcentre Plus office.

5. Challenging a decision

If you think a decision about your maternity allowance is wrong, you can ask the DWP to look at it again. This process is known as a 'mandatory reconsideration'. Provided you ask within the time limit (usually one month), the DWP notifies you of the decision in a 'mandatory reconsideration notice'. If you are still not happy when you get this notice, you can appeal to the independent First-tier Tribunal. If it was not possible to ask the DWP to reconsider the decision within a month, you can ask for a late revision (within 13 months), explaining why it is late. You can also ask the DWP to look at a decision again at any time if certain grounds are met – eg, if there has been an official error.

Chapter 9: Maternity, paternity and adoption benefits
6. Other benefits and tax credits

If you disagree with your employer's decision on your entitlement to statutory maternity, adoption, paternity or shared parental pay, or your employer fails to make a decision, you can ask HM Revenue and Customs to make a formal decision on your entitlement.

6. Other benefits and tax credits

There are a number of other benefits you may get when you have a baby, such as:
- child benefit when the baby is born;
- universal credit (UC), if you do not already get child tax credit (CTC) for other children you have, or working tax credit because you are working and on a low income;
- CTC in some cases, or an increase in your existing award. Tell HM Revenue and Customs within three months of the birth;
- in some cases, if you are 19 or under and in full-time non-advanced education or approved training on which you were accepted, enrolled or started before you turned 19, income support (IS) as a parent;
- in some cases, if you are a lone parent, IS whether or not you are a full-time student;
- a Best Start grant, if you are under 18 or get a qualifying benefit (see p114);
- Best Start foods, if you are under 18 or get a qualifying benefit (see p115).

Maternity allowance is taken into account when calculating whether the benefit cap applies (see p49 and p98). Statutory maternity, adoption, paternity and shared parental pay are not taken into account.

Chapter 10

Personal independence payment

This chapter covers:
1. What is personal independence payment (below)
2. Who is eligible (p86)
3. Amount of benefit (p87)
4. Claiming personal independence payment (p87)
5. Challenging a decision (p88)
6. Other benefits and tax credits (p88)

Basic facts
– Personal independence payment (PIP) is for people who need help with daily living or who have mobility difficulties.
– Part-time and full-time students can claim.
– If you are a full-time student, getting PIP helps you to be eligible for universal credit (although you must meet a medical test). In some cases, it also allows you to be eligible for income-related employment and support allowance and housing benefit.

1. What is personal independence payment

Personal independence payment (PIP) is a benefit for people with a disability. It is replacing disability living allowance (DLA) for people of working age (aged 16 to 64).

If you are already on DLA and are of working age, you will be assessed for PIP at some point. If you were 65 or over on 8 April 2013, you remain on DLA. If you are getting DLA and are of working age, you must claim PIP instead if you are invited to do so, or if your DLA award is due for renewal, you have a change of circumstances or if you turn 16.

PIP is not means tested, so it is not reduced because of your student support or other income. It comprises two components: for daily living and mobility. Each component has two rates: a standard rate and an enhanced rate.

2. Who is eligible

You qualify for personal independence payment (PIP) if you meet all the following conditions.
- You are aged 16 or over and, usually, under pension age.
- You satisfy certain rules on residence and presence in the UK, and are not a 'person subject to immigration control'. See CPAG's *Welfare Benefits and Tax Credits Handbook* for details.
- You satisfy the disability conditions for the daily living component and/or the mobility component.
- You have satisfied the disability conditions for the last three months (unless you are terminally ill) and are likely to continue to do so for the next nine months.

Your ability to undertake various activities is assessed, usually at a medical examination. Depending on the type and level of help you need, you score points on different activities. If you score eight points, you get the standard rate of a component; if you score 12 points, you get the enhanced rate. For example, if you cannot dress or undress yourself, you score eight points.

See CPAG's *Welfare Benefits and Tax Credits Handbook* for more information about the activities and the points awarded.

Daily living component

To get the standard rate of the daily living component, your ability to undertake certain specified day-to-day activities must be limited by your health or disability. To get the enhanced rate, your ability to undertake the activities must be severely limited.

You are assessed on your ability to carry out the following activities:
- preparing food. If you cannot prepare and cook a simple meal yourself, you can score points;
- taking nutrition;
- managing your therapy or monitoring your health condition;
- washing and bathing;
- managing your toilet needs or incontinence;
- dressing and undressing;
- communicating verbally. If you need to use an aid to help you speak or hear, you can score two points; if you need a British Sign Language interpreter to help you understand or express information, you can score four to eight points, depending on the help you need;
- reading and understanding signs, symbols and words. If you need help to read, or need to use an appliance or aid (other than glasses or contact lenses), you can score points;

- engaging face-to-face with other people;
- making budgeting decisions. You can score points if your disability means you need help with budgeting.

Mobility component

You get the standard rate of the mobility component if your ability to undertake certain mobility activities is limited by your health or disability. If your ability to undertake the activities is severely limited, you get the enhanced rate.

You are assessed on your ability to plan and follow journeys, and to move around. You can score points if you need help to follow an unfamiliar or familiar route, including if you can only do so with the help of a guide dog or orientation aid.

Students

If you are a part-time or full-time student, you can get PIP if you meet the qualifying conditions. Starting studying should not affect your award, provided you still have daily living and/or mobility needs.

3. Amount of benefit

Weekly rate from April 2019

Daily living component
Standard rate £58.70
Enhanced rate £87.65

Mobility component
Standard rate £23.20
Enhanced rate £61.20

4. Claiming personal independence payment

Phone 0800 917 2222 (textphone 0800 917 7777) to make a claim for personal independence payment (PIP). If you cannot claim by phone, you can ask for a claim form to be sent to you. Claims cannot be backdated, so claim as soon as you think you qualify.

When you phone, some basic information is taken from you. You are then sent a form on which to give more information about your condition and how it affects you. You must normally return this form within one month. You must then usually attend a medical assessment.

Chapter 10: Personal independence payment
6. Other benefits and tax credits

Awards of PIP are usually made for a fixed period – eg, two years or five years.
PIP is usually paid directly into your bank account, and is paid every four weeks in arrears.

5. Challenging a decision

If you think a decision about your personal independence payment is wrong, you can ask the DWP to look at it again. This process is known as a 'mandatory reconsideration'. Provided you ask within the time limit (usually one month), the DWP notifies you of the decision in a 'mandatory reconsideration notice'. If you are still not happy when you get this notice, you can appeal to the independent First-tier Tribunal. If it was not possible to ask the DWP to reconsider the decision within a month, you can ask for a late revision (within 13 months), explaining why it is late. You can also ask the DWP to look at a decision again at any time if certain grounds are met – eg, if there has been an official error.

6. Other benefits and tax credits

If you get personal independence payment (PIP) and are a student, this may help you to be eligible for universal credit (see p90). It can also allow you to get income-related employment and support allowance (ESA) and housing benefit (HB), although new claims for these benefits cannot usually be made (see p20 for ESA and p37 for HB).

If you claim other benefits or tax credits, make sure the office dealing with your claim knows you get PIP, as it may qualify you for additional amounts in these.

If you, your partner or a young person you are responsible for get PIP, you are exempt from the benefit cap (see p49 and p98).

Chapter 11

Universal credit

This chapter covers:
1. What is universal credit (below)
2. Who is eligible (p90)
3. Basic rules (p93)
4. Amount of benefit (p93)
5. Claiming universal credit (p97)
6. Challenging a decision (p98)
7. Other benefits and tax credits (p98)

> **Basic facts**
> – Universal credit (UC) is a new benefit, replacing means-tested benefits and tax credits.
> – Full-time students can qualify if they are a parent, have a non-student partner and in some other circumstances.
> – Part-time students who are able to meet their work-related requirements can qualify.
> – It can include amounts for adults, children, illness, caring responsibilities, rent and childcare costs.
> – You claim with your partner, and you are paid monthly in arrears in a single household payment.
> – The amount you get is usually affected by any grant, loan or other income you have.

1. What is universal credit

Universal credit (UC) is a new means-tested benefit for people of working age.

UC has now been rolled out in all areas, so you cannot usually make a new claim for a benefit or tax credit that UC is replacing and must claim UC instead (see p20, p37, p51, p68, p101 and p108). Once you claim UC, you remain on UC (provided you are still eligible), even if your circumstances change.

UC replaces the following benefits and tax credits:
- income support;
- income-based jobseeker's allowance;
- income-related employment and support allowance;

Chapter 11: Universal credit
2. Who is eligible

- housing benefit;
- child tax credit;
- working tax credit.

If you are a full-time student, you are only eligible for UC in some circumstances – broadly, if you are a parent, have a disability, if you are a young student in non-advanced education and without parental support, or if you have a partner who is not a student.

The amount you get is based on your circumstances (eg, whether you have a partner or child, or care for someone with a disability) and is usually affected by any grant, loan or other income you have.

2. Who is eligible

Students

To qualify for universal credit (UC), you must satisfy all the basic rules described on p93. Most students cannot claim UC, although there are some exceptions (see below). For UC, a student is referred to as someone 'receiving education'.

> *Receiving education*
> You are **'receiving education'** if you are:[1]
> – a qualifying young person. This applies if you are in non-advanced education of at least 12 hours a week and have not yet reached 31 August after your 19th birthday;
> – undertaking a full-time course of advanced education (see p52 – the rules are the same as for income support);[2]
> – on another full-time course for which a loan, grant or bursary is provided for your maintenance;
> – on a course that is not compatible with your 'work-related requirements' (ie, what you are expected to do in terms of looking for work) and you are not covered by the above three bullet points.
> You are 'undertaking a course' from the day you start the course until the last day of the course (or an earlier date when you abandon or are dismissed from the course).[3]

Who can claim universal credit

If you do not count as receiving education, you can claim UC in the same way as anyone else.

If you count as receiving education, you are only eligible for UC if you:[4]
- are responsible for a child or young person;
- are under 22 on a non-advanced course, you were under 21 when you started the course, and you are 'without parental support' (see p91);

- have limited capability for work and also get disability living allowance or personal independence payment. **Note:** if the DWP refuses to allow you to claim UC and be assessed for limited capability for work, you may be able to claim contributory employment and support allowance in order to establish your limited capability for work, and then claim UC once this has been established;
- are a single foster parent;
- are a member of a student couple and one of you is a foster parent;
- are over pension age and your partner has not yet reached that age;
- are making a joint claim with your partner who is not a student, or who is a student but would be eligible for UC her/himself while studying;
- have taken time out because of illness or caring responsibilities, you have now recovered or your caring responsibilities have ended, and you are not eligible for a grant or loan.

If you are in one of the above groups and have a partner who is also a student, you can make a joint claim for UC with her/him, even if s/he is not in one of these groups.[5]

Without parental support

'Without parental support' means you:[6]
- are an orphan; *or*
- cannot live with your parents because you are estranged from them, or because there is a serious risk to your physical or mental health, or you would face significant harm if you lived with them; *or*
- are living away from your parents, and they cannot support you financially because they are ill or disabled, in prison or not allowed to enter Great Britain.

Note: if you are aged 16 or 17 and receiving education, you can only claim UC if you are covered by one of the first three bullet points above – ie, you have a child, you are without parental support and in non-advanced education, or you are ill or disabled. If you are a 16/17-year-old care leaver and are receiving education, you can only claim if you have a child or are ill or disabled, and you cannot get help with housing costs.[7]

Examples
Jodie is 18 and on UC. She starts a full-time course of non-advanced education. She is estranged from her parents. She is still eligible for UC.

Lewis is on UC. He moves in with his partner Liz, who is on a full-time advanced course and has a three-year-old child. They are eligible for UC.

Chapter 11: Universal credit
2. Who is eligible

Pauline is 23 and is on UC. She starts a full-time non-advanced course. The DWP decides that her course is not compatible with her work-related requirements, so she counts as 'receiving education'. She is single and not disabled. She is not eligible for UC while she is on her course.

Karen is on UC. She moves in with her partner, Jake, who is unemployed. Karen starts a full-time advanced course. They are still eligible for UC.

Donna is a lone parent with a nine-year-old son. She is on housing benefit (HB) and child tax credit (CTC). In the summer vacation she claims UC and her HB and CTC stop.

Work-related requirements

Even if you are a student who can claim UC, you may have to meet certain 'work-related requirements' in order to get UC. These are set out in a 'claimant commitment', drawn up by your work coach at the job centre. If it is not possible to do so while on your course, you may be given a sanction and your UC may be reduced. See CPAG's *Welfare Benefits and Tax Credits Handbook* for more information about work-related requirements and sanctions.

There are no work-related requirements if you are receiving education and you are:[8]

- under 22 (and were under 21 when you started your course), in non-advanced education and have no parental support; *or*
- eligible for UC as a student (unless you are eligible after having taken time out because of illness or caring responsibilities) and you get a student loan for maintenance, or a maintenance grant that is taken into account for UC. This only applies during the period of the year in which your student income is taken into account. Normally, this is over the academic year (see Chapter 16). Over the summer vacation you may be subject to work-related requirements.

If you are not exempt from work-related requirements under the rules above and not exempt for any other reason (eg, because you have a child under one or you are severely disabled), you must meet your work-related requirements, otherwise you can be sanctioned. This means that your UC is reduced by the level of your standard allowance (see p94). You may be able to challenge a sanction. If you are given a sanction, get advice as soon as possible.

Examples

Sukhi is a full-time further education student. She gets a bursary maintenance allowance. She has a 12-year-old daughter. She claims UC. Because she gets a student grant for maintenance, no work-related requirements apply.

Sean is a lone parent with one child aged eight, studying a full-time Higher National Diploma course. He claims UC and does not have any work-related requirements applied because he gets a student loan. His long vacation starts on 12 June 2020. For the assessment period covering 13 June and the next two assessment periods, which are wholly within his summer vacation, he is subject to work-related requirements. If Sean cannot meet these requirements, he may be sanctioned and his UC reduced.

3. Basic rules

Universal credit (UC) is for people on a low income who are in or out of work. You can claim regardless of your circumstances, provided you meet the basic rules about age, education, residence, income and capital. So, for example, lone parents, people with a disability, carers and unemployed people can all claim UC. So if you are a student, you can only get UC if you meet the basic rules and are in one of the groups of student who are eligible for UC.

As well as being a student who is eligible to claim UC, you must satisfy all the following conditions.

- You are aged 18 or over. There are exceptions for some 16/17-year-olds – eg, if you are estranged from your parents, are a parent yourself, are sick or disabled or if you are caring for someone with a disability.
- You are under pension age (see p60). You can are also eligible if you have a partner who is over pension age, provided you are under pension age.
- You are in Great Britain, satisfy the 'habitual residence' and the 'right to reside' tests, and are not a 'person subject to immigration control'. These terms are explained in CPAG's *Welfare Benefits and Tax Credits Handbook*.
- You have no more than £16,000 capital.
- Your income is less than your 'maximum amount' of UC (see p94).
- You have agreed a 'claimant commitment', setting out what you must do to receive your UC. If you have a partner, you must each agree a claimant commitment to get benefit.

4. Amount of benefit

The amount of universal credit (UC) you get depends on your circumstances and the circumstances of your partner. The amount also depends on your and your partner's income and capital. Go through the following steps to work out the amount of UC to which you are entitled.

Step one: capital

If your capital is over £16,000, you cannot get UC. Some kinds of capital are ignored. For details, see CPAG's *Welfare Benefits and Tax Credits Handbook*.

Chapter 11: Universal credit
4. Amount of benefit

Step two: work out your maximum amount
Your maximum amount is worked out by adding together the monthly amounts of the standard allowance and any other elements for which you are eligible.

Step three: work out your monthly income
Chapter 16 explains how your loan, grant or other income is taken into account.

Step four: deduct monthly income from maximum amount
If your income is *less* than your maximum amount, UC is the difference between the two. If your income is *the same as or more than* your maximum amount, you cannot get UC.

Your maximum amount

Work out your maximum amount by adding together your standard allowance and any additional elements that apply. For the amounts, see pxi. The rates are monthly and are from April 2019.

Standard allowance
You get one standard allowance for yourself and any partner. There are different rates depending on whether you and your partner are under 25, or 25 or over.

Child element
You get one child element for each eligible dependent child who 'normally lives' with you.[9] Each child must be under 16, or aged 16 to 19 and in full-time non-advanced education or approved training.[10] You can only claim for a child up to 31 August following her/his 19th birthday, and s/he must have been under 19 when s/he started her/his education or training. You cannot claim for a child who claims UC, income support, jobseeker's allowance, employment and support allowance (ESA) or tax credits in her/his own right.

The higher child element is paid if one of your children was born before 6 April 2017.

You can usually only get a child element for a maximum of two children. However, you can get a child element for any child born before 6 April 2017. If you have a third child on or after 6 April 2017 and you get UC, you cannot get a child element for her/him unless an exception applies (see CPAG's *Welfare Benefits and Tax Credits Handbook* for what these are).

You get an additional amount for any child or young person who gets disability living allowance or personal independence payment, whether you get a child element for her/him or not. If the child is severely disabled, you get a higher amount.

Elements for illness

You get an extra amount of UC if you meet the test for 'limited capability for work' (the work capability assessment) and your claim (or your request to be assessed for limited capability for work) was made before 3 April 2017 or if you meet the test for 'limited capability for work-related activity'.

The work capability assessment is the same as that used for ESA to assess how much your health or disability limits your ability to work or undertake work-related activity.

Carer element

You qualify for a carer element if you are entitled to carer's allowance (CA), or you would be entitled to CA except for the fact that your earnings are too high. You must be caring for someone for at least 35 hours a week who is in receipt of certain disability benefits. You cannot get an element for being a carer and for your own illness at the same time.

Housing costs element

You get an amount for rent included in your UC if you are liable for the rent on your home (see below). If you own your home, you may be able to get help with certain service charges, but not if you have any earnings in an assessment period.

UC does not include amounts to cover your mortgage interest payments, but you may be able to get a loan from the DWP to help with these.

The housing element of UC for rent is paid directly to you, for you to then pay your landlord, although you can request for it to be paid directly to your landlord instead. See CPAG's *Welfare Benefits and Tax Credits Handbook* for more information.

An amount is deducted from your housing costs element if you are in rented accommodation and have a non-dependant living with you. This is called a 'housing costs contribution', and is a flat rate of £73.89 per month.

A non-dependant is someone, usually a friend or adult relative, who lives with you, but not on a commercial basis.

There is no deduction for a non-dependant who is under 21, and in certain other circumstances.

See CPAG's *Welfare Benefits and Tax Credits Handbook* for further details about the housing costs element, and about loans for mortgage interest.

Help with your rent

You must be liable for rent. There are some circumstances in which you can be treated as liable for the rent, even when you are not legally liable – eg, if you have taken over paying the rent from someone else.

Your UC housing costs element may not include the full amount of rent that you pay.

If you rent from a private landlord (including a hall of residence), your housing element is based on a standard 'local housing allowance' for the size of property that applies to you, even if your rent is higher than this amount. If your rent is lower, your housing element is based on the amount of your actual rent. Each local authority has its own rates for properties of different sizes. Check your local authority's rates at http://lha-direct.voa.gov.uk/search.aspx.

Generally, you are allowed one bedroom for:
- an adult couple;
- another single adult aged 16 or over;
- two children under 16 of the same sex;
- two children under 10;
- any other child.

You are allowed a maximum of four bedrooms. If you are a single person aged under 35 with no children, the local housing allowance is usually a lower, shared-accommodation rate. If you are disabled and need overnight care, you may qualify for an additional bedroom for a carer. See CPAG's *Welfare Benefits and Tax Credits Handbook* for details.

If you rent from a local authority or housing association, your housing element is usually the same as the weekly rent due. However, it is reduced if you are considered to have a spare bedroom (known as the 'bedroom tax'). The rules about how many bedrooms you can have are similar to the local housing allowance rules, but see CPAG's *Welfare Benefits and Tax Credits Handbook* for more information. If you are considered to have one spare bedroom, the reduction is 14 per cent, and 25 per cent if you have two or more spare bedrooms. If your housing element is reduced in this way, you should apply for a discretionary housing payment from the local authority.

A **discretionary housing payment** can be paid if you get UC that includes a housing costs element and you need additional help with your housing costs – eg, to make up the shortfall in rent due to your housing element being reduced because you have a spare bedroom. Payments are usually awarded for a temporary period, beyond which you have to reapply. Apply to your local authority.

Childcare element

If you are working, you can get help with up to 85 per cent of your childcare costs, up to a maximum monthly amount. You must be in paid work, but there is no minimum number of hours that you must work. If you have a partner, you must both be in paid work, unless your partner is ill or disabled, or a carer.

> **Example**
> Chloe is 22 and her partner Jo is 23. They are unemployed and get UC. Chloe starts a full-time, two-year Higher National Diploma course. She gets a student loan of £6,750, plus an independent students' bursary of £1,000.
> **During the academic year September 2019 to May 2020:**
> Step one Chloe and Jo have no savings or capital.
> Step two Their maximum amount of UC is:
>   Standard allowance for a couple under 25 £395.20
>   Housing costs £398.00
>   Total £793.20
> Step three Their monthly income is:
>   Chloe's student loan £733.75
>   The independent students' bursary is disregarded. The loan is divided over eight months of the academic year, and £110 of the remaining amount is disregarded (see Chapter 16).
> Step four Their income is below their maximum amount, so they get UC of £59.45 per month.
>
> **From May 2020 to September 2020:**
> Step two Chloe and Jo's maximum amount of UC is still £793.20 (at 2019/20 rates).
> Step three Their weekly income for UC purposes is nil. This is because Chloe's student income only counts until the assessment period before the summer vacation.
> Step four From May 2020 to September 2020, their monthly UC is £793.20, so they get maximum UC from May to September.

5. Claiming universal credit

You usually make a claim for universal credit (UC) online at www.gov.uk/apply-universal-credit. Help with online claims over the telephone, telephone claims and face-to-face claims should also be possible if required. If you have a partner, you claim jointly with her/him. You may be able to get help to make your claim from a local Citizens Advice office.

The DWP administers UC, and payments are made monthly in arrears. In Scotland, payments can be made twice-monthly and rent amounts can be paid directly to your landlord.[11] In exceptional circumstances, you can request alternative payment arrangements – eg, to get paid more regularly, or to get the payment split between you and your partner. This is a discretionary decision. See CPAG's *Welfare Benefits and Tax Credits Handbook* for more information.

Chapter 11: Universal credit
7. Other benefits and tax credits

If you are an employee, you do not usually need to report any changes in your earnings, as HM Revenue and Customs provides this information directly to the DWP.

If you do not have enough money to live on while you are waiting for your first payment of UC, you can ask for an advance payment. This can be for up to 100 per cent of your award, and you repay it over the subsequent 12 months.

UC advances can also be made when your needs have increased and you are waiting for an extra element of UC to be paid with your next monthly regular payment – eg, when you first have a new baby or become responsible for a child. Awards are at the DWP's discretion. You must repay an advance, usually from the next three months' UC payments.

You can also ask for a loan, called a budgeting advance of UC, to meet certain needs once you have been getting UC for six months. Budgeting advances of UC must normally be repaid from your next 12 months' UC payments. See CPAG's *Welfare Benefits and Tax Credits Handbook* for more information.

6. Challenging a decision

If you think a decision about your universal credit is wrong, you can ask the DWP to look at it again. This process is known as a 'mandatory reconsideration'. Provided you ask within the time limit (usually one month), the DWP notifies you of the decision in a 'mandatory reconsideration notice'. If you are still not happy when you get this notice, you can appeal to the independent First-tier Tribunal. If it was not possible to ask the DWP to reconsider the decision within a month, you can ask for a late revision (within 13 months), explaining why it is late. You can also ask the DWP to look at a decision again at any time if certain grounds are met – eg, if there has been an official error.

7. Other benefits and tax credits

You cannot make a new claim for income support, income-based jobseeker's allowance (JSA), income-related employment and support allowance (ESA), housing benefit (there are some exceptions – see p37), child tax credit or working tax credit, unless you have a severe disability premium in one of these benefits already (or you got one in the last month and still satisfy the conditions for it).

You can still get other benefits, such as carer's allowance (CA), contributory ESA or contribution-based JSA, but they may count as income.

The benefit cap

Your universal credit (UC) is reduced if your total income from benefits is over the maximum level that you or your partner can receive. The amount is £1,666.66 a month if you are a lone parent or member of a couple, and £1,116.66 if you are a single person.

The benefits that count towards the cap include child benefit and maternity allowance.

You are exempt from the cap if:
- you or your partner are working and earning at least £430 a month;
- you or your partner are disabled. You or your partner must get certain disability benefits, including disability living allowance (DLA), personal independence payment (PIP), ESA with a support component, or UC with a limited capability for work-related activity element;
- you are responsible for a child or young person who gets DLA or PIP;
- you or your partner are a carer and get CA or the carer element in UC;
- you are a war widow/er.

There is protection for nine months before the cap applies if you are no longer working, or are earning less than £430 a month, but were working and earning at least £430 a month for each of the 12 months before this.

Passported benefits

Provided you meet any other conditions, getting UC entitles you to:
- a Best Start grant;
- funeral support payments;
- free school lunches from your local authority, provided your earnings (or the earnings of you and your partner) are not more than £610 in the assessment period before your application.

If you get UC and have income below a certain level, you are eligible for:
- free dental treatment (see p32);
- vouchers for glasses (see p32);
- Best Start foods (see p115).

Chapter 11: Universal credit
Notes

2. Who is eligible
1 Reg 12 UC Regs
2 paras H6031 and H6047 ADM
3 Reg 13(1) UC Regs
4 Regs 3(2)(b), 13(4) and 14 UC Regs
5 Reg 3(2)(b) UC Regs
6 Reg 8(3) UC Regs
7 Reg 8 and Sch 4 para 4 UC Regs
8 Reg 89 UC Regs

4. Amount of benefit
9 Reg 4(2) UC Regs
10 Reg 5 UC Regs

5. Claiming universal credit
11 The Universal Credit (Claims and Payments) (Scotland) Regulations 2017, No.227

Chapter 12
Child tax credit

This chapter covers:
1. What is child tax credit (below)
2. Who is eligible (p102)
3. Amount of child tax credit (p103)
4. Claiming child tax credit (p105)
5. Challenging a decision (p106)
6. Tax credits and benefits (p106)

> **Basic facts**
> – Child tax credit is paid to families with children.
> – Both part-time and full-time students with children are eligible.
> – The amount you get depends on your income, but most student support is ignored in the assessment.

1. What is child tax credit

Child tax credit (CTC) is a payment made to people with children. It is administered by HM Revenue and Customs and paid whether you are working or not working. Full-time and part-time students with children are eligible. You get a higher amount if you have a child with a disability. The amount of CTC depends on your income in the tax year.

Note: you cannot usually make a new claim for CTC, as it is in the process of being replaced by universal credit. However, an exception applies if you get, or got in the past month (and continue to satisfy the rules for it), a severe disability premium in your income support, income-based jobseeker's allowance, income-related employment and support allowance or housing benefit. If you already get CTC, you can add working tax credit to your award and vice versa.

Chapter 12: Child tax credit
2. Who is eligible

2. Who is eligible

As new claims cannot usually be made (see above for exceptions), most students getting child tax credit (CTC) will be those who were already on CTC (and/or working tax credit) before starting the course. If you cannot claim CTC then you may be able to get universal credit instead (see Chapter 11).

You are eligible for CTC if you meet all the following conditions.[1]
- You are aged 16 or over.
- You have a dependent child. You can get CTC for a child until 1 September after her/his 16th birthday. If s/he stays on at school, in other full-time non-advanced education or is on approved training (defined as 'Employability Fund activity'), you can get CTC for her/him until her/his 19th, or sometimes 20th, birthday.[2] This includes during gaps between one course ending and another starting, provided the young person starts the next course. You can only continue to get CTC for a 19-year-old on a course or training which s/he was accepted on, enrolled on, or started before s/he reached 19 until s/he leaves the course or turns 20, whichever is earlier. You may be able to continue to get CTC for a young person under age 18 for 20 weeks after s/he leaves non-advanced education if s/he notifies HM Revenue and Customs (HMRC) within three months that s/he has registered for work or training with Skills Development Scotland. If your child lives with someone else part of the time, you should decide between you who has main responsibility, otherwise HMRC decides who gets CTC.
- You are 'present and ordinarily resident' in Britain, are not a 'person subject to immigration control' and have a 'right to reside'. You must normally have been living in the UK for three months before you claim. These terms are explained in CPAG's *Welfare Benefits and Tax Credits Handbook*. Overseas students can get further advice from UKCISA (see Appendix 2).
- Your income is not too high (see Chapter 18).

There are no special rules for students. Both part-time and full-time students are eligible.

Your parent gets child tax credit for you

If you live with your parent(s), s/he cannot get CTC for you if you are in higher education. S/he can continue to get CTC for you until your 19th, or sometimes 20th, birthday if you are in full-time non-advanced education (see above). The course must be one recognised by the Scottish government and be more than 12 hours a week, on average, in term time. The course hours include tuition, supervised study, exams, practical work and any exercise or project in the curriculum. Do not count meal breaks or unsupervised study. You count as full time between courses if you are enrolled on another non-advanced course.

Your parent(s) cannot get CTC for you if you get universal credit, income support, income-based jobseeker's allowance, employment and support allowance, CTC or working tax credit in your own right.

If you live with a partner, or are married or in a civil partnership, your parent(s) can only get CTC for you if your partner is also a young person in full-time non-advanced education or approved training.

In some circumstances, special rules apply – eg, if you are being looked after by a local authority or are in prison or a young offenders' institution.

3. Amount of child tax credit

The amount of child tax credit (CTC) you get if you are not working and eligible for working tax credit (WTC) depends on your family circumstances (your 'maximum CTC') and how much income you have. If you are eligible for WTC (see Chapter 13), you claim both tax credits together and the amount is worked out together. Tax credits are calculated according to a maximum annual amount that you could receive in the tax year (6 April – 5 April). However, often an annual award is worked out by adding together amounts calculated over separate periods within the year because, for example, you start a new claim or your circumstances change – eg, you have another child, you cease to be a member of a couple or you start work or increase your hours. What follows, therefore, is a simplification of what is often a very complicated calculation and assumes you are claiming CTC (but not WTC) for a full tax year and have no changes in your circumstances during that year. See CPAG's *Welfare Benefits and Tax Credits Handbook* for the detailed rules.

HM Revenue and Customs (HMRC) has a tax credits calculator at www.gov.uk/tax-credits-calculator, where you can check how much CTC you are likely to get.

Step one: work out your maximum child tax credit
The maximum CTC you can get is made up of:
- **child element** of £2,780 a year for each child. **Note:** you cannot get a child element for a child born on or after 6 April 2017 if you are already claiming for two or more children. There are exceptions (see CPAG's *Welfare Benefits and Tax Credits Handbook* for these); *plus*
- **family element** of £545 a year. You only get this if your claim includes a child born before 6 April 2017; *plus*
- **disabled child element** of £3,355 a year for each child who gets disability living allowance (DLA), personal independence payment (PIP) or is certified as severely sight impaired or blind; *plus*
- **severely disabled child element** of £1,360 a year for each child who gets the highest rate care component of DLA or the enhanced rate daily living component of PIP.

Chapter 12: Child tax credit
3. Amount of child tax credit

These are the maximum amounts for the tax year April 2019 to April 2020. You get less than the maximum if your income is above a set threshold.

Example
Mairi has two children: Daisy, aged two, and Meena, aged four. Meena has asthma and gets the lowest rate care component of DLA. Mairi's maximum CTC for the tax year April 2019 to April 2020 is:

	£
Two child elements	2,780
	2,780
Family element	545
Disabled child element	3,355
Total maximum CTC	**9,460**

Whether she gets maximum CTC or a reduced amount depends on her income.

If your circumstances change so that you should gain or lose an element, tell HMRC so your award can be adjusted. If you should gain an element (eg, you have a new baby), you must tell HMRC within one month, otherwise you do not get the increase fully backdated. The exception to this is that the disabled child element and the severely disabled child elements can be fully backdated if you notify HMRC within one month of the DLA or PIP being awarded.

Other changes must be notified within one month – eg, if you stop being part of a couple. For details, see CPAG's *Welfare Benefits and Tax Credits Handbook*.

Step two: getting a means-tested benefit

You automatically get maximum CTC if you are getting income support (IS), income-based jobseeker's allowance (JSA), income-related employment and support allowance (ESA) or pension credit (PC).

Step three: not getting a means-tested benefit

If you do not get IS, income-based JSA, income-related ESA or PC, you must compare your income with a set threshold. The income threshold is £16,105, unless you are working and eligible for WTC. If your income is the same as or below this, you get maximum CTC. If your income is above this threshold, you get a reduced amount. If you or your partner are working and you are eligible for WTC, the income threshold is £6,420 instead of £16,105 (and Step one includes WTC elements).

Step four: work out your income

How your student income is calculated for tax credits is covered in Chapter 18. A CTC award for a tax year is usually based on your income in the previous tax year. However, if you expect your income over the current tax year to be more than

£2,500 lower or higher than the previous year, tell HMRC and it reassesses your tax credits. Your award is then based on the current year's income plus £2,500 if it is more than £2,500 lower than in the previous year, or based on the current year's income minus £2,500 if it is more than £2,500 higher than the previous year's award.

Step five: calculate your child tax credit
If your income is less than or the same as the threshold, you get maximum CTC. If your income is higher than the threshold, work out 41 per cent of the difference. Your CTC is the amount worked out at Step one minus 41 per cent of the difference between your income and the threshold.

Note: this simplified calculation gives an approximate amount of CTC. Amounts are actually calculated using daily rates. See CPAG's *Welfare Benefits and Tax Credits Handbook* for more details.

4. Claiming child tax credit

If you can make a new claim for tax credits (see p101), you do so by phoning the Tax Credit Helpline (see below).

When completing the form, remember to describe your circumstances, such as how many children you have or how many hours you work as they stand at the time of your claim, but you must list your income as it was in the previous tax year. Bear in mind that HM Revenue and Customs (HMRC) requires your income for a tax year, April to April, even though your student award may run from September.

> **Contacting HM Revenue and Customs**
> You can report changes of circumstances or make enquiries to the Tax Credit Helpline on 0345 300 3900 (textphone 0345 300 3909) between 8am and 8pm, Monday to Friday, and 8am and 4pm on Saturdays. It is often very difficult to get through to the Helpline.

Your claim can be backdated for up to one month. Your award runs until the end of the tax year, at which point you are sent a renewal form. Your award can change or end during the year. Tell HMRC about changes in your circumstances. You should also tell HMRC if you expect your income that counts for tax credits to decrease by more than £2,500 in the current tax year, or if you expect it to increase by more than £2,500.

Tax credits are paid directly into a bank account.

Chapter 12: Child tax credit
6. Tax credits and benefits

5. Challenging a decision

If you think a decision about your child tax credit is wrong, you can ask HM Revenue and Customs (HMRC) to look at it again. This process is known as a 'mandatory reconsideration'. Provided you ask within the time limit (usually 30 days), HMRC notifies you of the decision in a 'mandatory reconsideration notice'. If you are still not happy when you get this notice, you can appeal to the independent First-tier Tribunal. If it was not possible to ask HMRC to reconsider the decision within 30 days, you can ask for a late review (within 13 months), explaining why it is late. You can also ask HMRC to look at a decision again at any time if certain grounds are met – eg, if there has been an official error.

If you want to complain about the way your claim has been dealt with, write to the Tax Credit Office, BX9 1ER.

If you have been overpaid, the leaflet COP26, *What Happens if We've Paid You Too Much Tax Credits*, explains when the overpayment can be written off and what you need to do. HMRC sets out what you are expected to do to ensure your claim is correct and what you can expect of HMRC. If you have met all your responsibilities and HMRC has failed to meet one of its, the overpayment should not be recovered. This leaflet also explains when you can ask to repay an amount owed over a longer period. If an overpayment is challenged, it should not be recovered until the dispute is resolved. If you want to dispute recovery of an overpayment, HMRC expects you to do so within three months.

6. Tax credits and benefits

Means-tested benefits

Child tax credit (CTC) is not taken into account as income for income support, income-based jobseeker's allowance or income-related employment and support allowance, although working tax credit (WTC) is.

Tax credits are taken into account as income for housing benefit. If a tax credit overpayment from a previous year is being deducted, the amount of the tax credit award less the deduction is taken into account. If you have been overpaid in the same year as the award and the tax credit award is consequently reduced, the lower amount of the award still to be paid to you is taken into account.

Arrears of tax credits are treated as capital for means-tested benefits and disregarded for 52 weeks.

CTC is taken into account when calculating whether the benefit cap applies (see p49). If you or your partner get WTC, the benefit cap does not apply.

Chapter 12: Child tax credit
Notes

Child benefit

Child benefit is paid in addition to tax credits. It is ignored as income in the tax credit assessment.

Passported benefits

Getting CTC or WTC may entitle you to other benefits. You may be able to get the following.
- Free school lunches from the local authority. Your income for tax credit purposes must be no more than £16,105 a year. You must get CTC but not be eligible for WTC, unless your income for tax credit purposes is no more than £6,900, or you are getting the four-week run-on of WTC because you have reduced your hours or stopped work.[3]
- Health benefits, such as free dental treatment and vouchers for glasses. Your income for tax credit purposes must be no more than £15,276 and you must be getting CTC or WTC with a disability element. See Chapter 5 for other ways to qualify for health benefits.
- Best Start grants and funeral support payments. You qualify if you get CTC or WTC (or both). See https://cpag.org.uk/scotland/welfare-rights/scottish-benefits for more information.
- Best Start foods. If you have a child under three, or you are pregnant, and get CTC but are not entitled to WTC (except during the four-week run-on period) and have an annual income for tax credit purposes of no more than £16,190, you may be eligible for a Best Start foods payment card which can be used to buy certain foods. You are also eligible if you get WTC (with or without CTC) and have an annual income for tax credit purposes of under £7,320.[4]

Notes

2. **Who is eligible**
   1 Regs 3-5 CTC Regs
   2 Reg 5 CTC Regs

6. **Tax credits and benefits**
   3 The Education (School Lunches) (Scotland) Regulations 2009, No.178
   4 Reg 10 The Welfare Foods (Best Start Foods) (Scotland) Regulations 2019, No.193

Chapter 13
Working tax credit

This chapter covers:
1. What is working tax credit (below)
2. Who is eligible (p109)
3. Amount of working tax credit (p110)
4. Claiming working tax credit (p112)
5. Challenging a decision (p113)
6. Tax credits and benefits (p113)

> **Basic facts**
> – Working tax credit (WTC) is paid to top up low wages.
> – Both part-time and full-time students are eligible.
> – You may be eligible if you are over 25 and working at least 30 hours a week.
> – You may be eligible if you are working at least 16 or 24 hours a week and you have a child, a disability or are over 60.
> – You can get help with childcare costs in your WTC.
> – The amount you get depends on your income, but most student support is ignored in the assessment.

1. What is working tax credit

Working tax credit (WTC) helps supplement low wages. It is administered by HM Revenue and Customs. It is paid to people who are working (employed or self-employed) for at least 16 hours a week or, in some cases, 24 or 30 hours a week. Full-time and part-time students are eligible. You get a higher amount if you work 30 hours a week or have a disability. You can get childcare costs paid with WTC. The amount of WTC you get depends on your income in the tax year.

Note: you cannot usually make a new claim for WTC, as it is in the process of being replaced by universal credit. However, an exception applies if you get, or got in the past month (and continue to satisfy the rules for it), a severe disability premium (see p27) in your income support, income-based jobseeker's allowance, income-related employment and support allowance or housing benefit. If you already get WTC you can add child tax credit to your award, and vice versa.

Chapter 13: Working tax credit
2. Who is eligible

2. Who is eligible

As new claims cannot usually be made (see p108 for exceptions), most students getting working tax credit (WTC) will be those who were already on WTC (and/or child tax credit) before starting the course. If you cannot claim WTC, you may be able to get universal credit instead (see Chapter 11).

You qualify for WTC if you meet all of the following conditions.
- You are working sufficient hours and have a child or a disability, or you meet certain age conditions (see below).
- You are 'present and ordinarily resident' in the UK and not a 'person subject to immigration control'. These terms are explained in CPAG's *Welfare Benefits and Tax Credits Handbook*.
- Your income is not too high (see p112).

There are no special rules for students. Both part-time and full-time students are eligible.

Qualifying hours

To get WTC, you must work sufficient hours and meet other conditions. There are four ways to qualify.[1]
- **You have a child living with you.** You are eligible if:
  – you are aged 16 or over; *and*
  – you are working at least 16 hours a week and you are single or your partner is incapacitated, in hospital or prison, or gets carer's allowance, or you are a member of a couple and you are working at least 16 hours a week and between you and your partner you are working at least 24 hours a week; *and*
  – you have a dependent child. The rules are the same as for child tax credit (see p102).
- **You are a disabled worker.** You are eligible if:
  – you are aged 16 or over; *and*
  – you are working 16 hours or more a week; *and*
  – you have a disability that puts you at a disadvantage in getting a job and you pass a disability benefit test. If you are unable to satisfy one of a list of activities or functions about your mobility, manual dexterity, vision, hearing, speech, fits and mental disability, and about any severe pain and rehabilitation, you pass the disadvantage test. HM Revenue and Customs (HMRC) may contact a doctor or medical professional to confirm this. You pass the disability benefit test if you get certain benefits such as disability living allowance or personal independence payment, or in the past six months you have been getting other benefits such as the higher rate of short-term or long-term incapacity benefit, employment and support allowance for at least 28 weeks, or a disability premium in a means-tested benefit. For

more details, see CPAG's *Welfare Benefits and Tax Credits Handbook*. The test is also detailed in the notes for the claim form, TC600.
- **You are over 25.** You are eligible if:
  – you are aged 25 or over; *and*
  – you are working 30 hours or more a week.
- **You are over 60.** You are eligible if:
  – you are aged 60 or over; *and*
  – you are working 16 hours or more a week.

In each case, the work you do must be paid work. It must be expected to continue for at least four weeks from the time you claim WTC. This means you can claim WTC for work during long vacations but not during short vacations unless you will be working for at least four weeks. You can also claim during term time if you normally work sufficient hours to qualify. You must tell HMRC when you stop work, or if your hours reduce below the level required to qualify for WTC. In either case, your WTC award continues for another four weeks (called the 'four-week run-on').

3. Amount of working tax credit

The amount of working tax credit (WTC) you get depends on your circumstances (your 'maximum WTC') and how much income you have. Tax credits are calculated according to a maximum annual amount that you could receive in the tax year (6 April – 5 April). However, often awards must be calculated on part years because of changes in your circumstances – eg, you have another child, you cease to be a member of a couple or you change your hours of work. What follows, therefore, is a simplification of what is often a very complicated calculation and assumes you are claiming for a full tax year and have no changes in your circumstances during that year. See CPAG's *Welfare Benefits and Tax Credits Handbook* for the detailed rules.

The government website has tax credit pages at www.gov.uk/topic/benefits-credits/tax-credits. You can use these to check whether you qualify and how much WTC you are likely to get.

The way in which WTC is calculated is the same as for child tax credit (CTC – see p103), except that the threshold with which your income is compared is always £6,420. First, work out your maximum WTC (and add the maximum CTC, if applicable). Then work out your income (see Chapter 18). Use your income for the previous tax year, unless the current year's income is more than £2,500 lower (in which case use the current year's income plus £2,500), or more than £2,500 higher (in which case use the current year's income minus £2,500) than this. Finally, work out 41 per cent of the amount by which your income exceeds £6,420, and subtract this from your maximum WTC.

Chapter 13: Working tax credit
3. Amount of working tax credit

Note: this simplified calculation gives an approximate amount of WTC. Amounts are actually calculated using daily rates. See CPAG's *Welfare Benefits and Tax Credits Handbook* for more details.

The maximum WTC you can get is made up of a **basic element** of £1,960 a year plus whichever one or more of the following elements apply:
- **lone parent/couple element** of £2,010 a year;
- **30-hour element** of £810 a year if you work at least 30 hours a week (you can add your hours to your partner's if you have a child);
- **disabled worker element** of £3,165 a year if you qualify for WTC as a disabled worker (see p109);
- **severe disability element** of £1,365 a year if you get the highest rate care component of disability living allowance (DLA) or the enhanced rate of the daily living component of personal independence payment;
- **childcare element**. You can get up to 70 per cent of your childcare costs up to a limit of £175 a week for one child or £300 for two or more children – ie, a maximum of £122.50 or £210. The childcare must be of a certain type, including a registered childminder, nursery or playscheme, an out-of-hours club or sitters service. You do not get help with childcare at home provided by a relative. To get the childcare element you must be a lone parent, or a couple and either both of you are working 16 hours or more a week, or one of you is incapacitated, in hospital or in prison.

These are the amounts for the tax year April 2019 to April 2020. The maximum amounts usually go up each April. You will get less than the maximum if your income is more than a set threshold.

Examples
Sian is 26 and gets CTC. She does not work during the academic year, but in the summer vacation she gets a job for 30 hours a week and expects to work for nine weeks. Sian is eligible for WTC. Whether any WTC is payable depends on the level of her wages and other income.

Katherine and Spencer have a four-year-old child at nursery school. Katherine is a student and Spencer works 24 hours a week. Katherine works 16 hours a week during the summer only. They are eligible for WTC throughout the year. During the summer they can get a 30-hour element included in their WTC and they can also claim help with nursery charges.

Morag is a full-time student on a Higher National Certificate course. She has an eight-year-old daughter. She works 20 hours a week. Her income is a student loan, lone parents' grant of £1,305, and earnings of £7,800 in the tax year April 2019 to April 2020. In the previous tax year 2018/19, she worked full time and earned £15,000.

Chapter 13: Working tax credit
4. Claiming working tax credit

Her maximum tax credits are:

	£
CTC family element	545
CTC child element	2,780
WTC basic element	1,960
WTC lone parent element	2,010
Total maximum tax credits	**7,295**

Her income this year is more than £2,500 lower than last year when she was working full time, so this year's income plus £2,500 is used.
Her income is £7,800 + £2,500 + £1,305 = £11,605
(Her student loan is ignored – see Chapter 18.)
The threshold is £6,420.
Income minus threshold is £11,605 – £6,420 = £5,185
41% x £5,185 = £2,125.85
Maximum tax credits of £7,295 is reduced by £2,125.85.
Morag gets tax credits of £5,169.15, or about £99 a week.

The income threshold is £6,420. If your income is below this you get maximum WTC. If your income is above this threshold, you get a reduced amount. See Chapter 18 for what income counts in the assessment.

If your circumstances change so that you could gain or lose an element, tell HM Revenue and Customs (HMRC) so your award can be adjusted. If you should gain an element (eg, because your hours of work increase or you incur eligible childcare costs), you must tell HMRC within one month, otherwise you do not get the increase fully backdated. The exception to this is that the disabled worker element or severe disability element can be fully backdated if you notify HMRC within one month of DLA being awarded.

Some changes must be reported within one month – eg, if you stop working.

4. Claiming working tax credit

If you can make a new claim for tax credits (see p108), you do so by phoning the Tax Credit Helpline on 0345 300 3900 (textphone 0345 300 3909).

Your claim can be backdated for up to one month.

Any childcare element of working tax credit (WTC) is paid to the main carer directly into a bank account. Otherwise WTC is paid into the bank account of the person in work.

When you claim, the form asks for your income in the previous tax year (see Chapter 18). Your income might be very different this year. When you get your initial award, tell HM Revenue and Customs straight away how much your income is expected to be in the current year if it will be more than £2,500 lower or more than £2,500 higher than the previous year.

5. Challenging a decision

If you think a decision about your working tax credit is wrong, you can ask HM Revenue and Customs (HMRC) to look at it again. This process is known as a 'mandatory reconsideration'. Provided you ask within the time limit (usually 30 days), HMRC notifies you of the decision in a 'mandatory reconsideration notice'. If you are still not happy when you get this notice, you can appeal to the independent First-tier Tribunal. If it was not possible to ask HMRC to reconsider the decision within 30 days, you can ask for a late review (within 13 months), explaining why it is late. You can also ask HMRC to look at a decision again at any time if certain grounds are met – eg, if there has been an official error.

If HMRC has overpaid you, see p106.

6. Tax credits and benefits

If you or your partner get working tax credit (WTC), the benefit cap does not apply.

See p106 for details of how WTC affects benefits.

See p107 for details of the passported benefits you may be eligible for if you get WTC.

Notes

2. Who is eligible
1   Reg 4 The Working Tax Credit (Entitlement and Maximum Rate) Regulations 2002, No.2005

Chapter 14

Other payments

This chapter covers:
1. Best Start grants (below)
2. Best Start foods (p115)
3. Funeral support payments (p115)
4. Budgeting loans (p116)
5. The Scottish Welfare Fund (p117)
6. Challenging a decision (p117)

Basic facts
– To qualify for a Best Start grant, Best Start foods and funeral support payments, you must usually receive a qualifying benefit.
– Budgeting loans from the social fund are for people who get a qualifying benefit.
– You may be eligible for help from the Scottish Welfare Fund if you get a qualifying benefit or are on a low income.
– Students are eligible for these payments in the same way as anyone else.

1. Best Start grants

If you are pregnant or have a young child, you may be entitled to a Best Start grant. There are three separate one-off payments available.[1] These are:
- a pregnancy and baby payment of £600 if it is your first child, or £300 for a second or subsequent child. You can apply from the 24th week of pregnancy until six months after the baby is born;
- an early learning payment of £250 if you have a child aged between two and three-and-a-half years old;
- a school age payment of £250 in the year your child would normally start school.

You are eligible for these payments if you are under 18 or get a qualifying benefit. You are also eligible if you are 18 or 19 and someone else claims child benefit,

universal credit (UC), child tax credit (CTC) or pension credit for you. There are no special rules for students. Qualifying benefits are:
- UC (including if you got UC in the last month and it has now stopped);
- income support;
- income-based jobseeker's allowance;
- income-related employment and support allowance;
- pension credit;
- housing benefit;
- CTC;
- working tax credit.

See https://cpag.org.uk/scotland/welfare-rights/scottish-social-security for more details. You can apply online, by phone on 0800 182 2222 or by downloading a paper form. Go to www.mygov.scot/get-help-applying-best-start-grant-foods for more information or to start an application.

2. Best Start foods

You can get a payment card to buy certain foods under the Best Start foods scheme if you are pregnant or have a child under three and you get a qualifying benefit, or if you are under 18.

Qualifying benefits are:[2]
- universal credit (if you have earnings, they must be under £610 a month);
- income support;
- income-based jobseeker's allowance;
- income-related employment and support allowance;
- pension credit;
- housing benefit (if you have income under £311 a week);
- child tax credit (if you have income under £16,190);
- working tax credit (if you have income under £7,320 a year).

3. Funeral support payments

At the time of writing, from summer 2019 funeral support payments were due to replace social fund funeral payments in Scotland. See https://cpag.org.uk/cpag-scotland/welfare-rights-scotland/scottish-benefits/funeral-support-payment for more details and up-to-date information about when these payments are introduced.

Funeral support payments are to help with burial or cremation costs for a partner, family member or friend. It has to be reasonable for you to accept

Chapter 14: Other payments
5. The Scottish Welfare Fund

responsibility for the costs, and this requires looking at factors including whether it is more reasonable for someone closer to the person who has died to take responsibility. There are no special rules for students.

You must get one of the following qualifying benefits:[3]
- universal credit (including if you got this in the last month and it has now stopped);
- income support;
- income-based jobseeker's allowance;
- income-related employment and support allowance;
- pension credit;
- housing benefit;
- child tax credit; *or*
- working tax credit.

Note: until funeral support payments are introduced, you can still apply for social fund funeral payments. See the previous edition of this *Handbook* for more information.

4. Budgeting loans

You can get a budgeting loan to help you pay for certain items – eg, furniture, clothes, removal expenses, rent in advance, home improvements, travelling expenses, maternity expenses, funeral expenses and jobseeking expenses. If you are claiming universal credit, you must apply for a budgeting advance instead of a budgeting loan (see p97). There are no special rules for students.

The amount of budgeting loan you can get depends on the size of your family and how long you have been on benefit. To qualify, you must have been getting one of the following for at least 26 weeks before your claim is decided:
- income support;
- income-based jobseeker's allowance;
- income-related employment and support allowance; *or*
- pension credit.

See CPAG's *Welfare Benefits and Tax Credits Handbook* for details of who can get a loan and how to apply.

5. The Scottish Welfare Fund

Local authorities administer the Scottish Welfare Fund. This comprises community care grants to help people remain in or establish themselves in the community and crisis grants for people without money because of a disaster or emergency. To qualify, you must be on a low income. You may get a crisis grant, for example, if you are on a low income and there has been a disaster like a fire or a flood, or you have lost money that you needed to live on. Students are not excluded from applying to the Scottish Welfare Fund. More information, including how to apply, is at www.mygov.scot/scottish-welfare-fund.

6. Challenging a decision

If you think a decision about your Best Start grant or funeral support payment is wrong, you can ask Social Security Scotland (SSS) to look at it again. This process is known as a 'redetermination'. The time limit is usually one month from the decision being notified to you. If you are still not happy when you get the further decision, you can appeal to the independent First-tier Tribunal. If it was not possible to ask SSS to redetermine the decision within 31 days, you can ask for a late redetermination (within one year), explaining why it is late.

You can ask for a review of a budgeting loan decision within 28 days of the day the decision was issued to you (or sometimes later, if you have special reasons or if there is a mistake in the decision about the law or the facts of your case).

You can ask for a review of a Scottish Welfare Fund decision within 20 days (or later if you have good reasons for asking for this late). If you are still not happy, you can ask for the decision to be looked at again by the Scottish Public Services Ombudsman (www.spso.org.uk).

Notes

1. **Best Start grants**
   1 The Early Years Assistance (Best Start Grants) (Scotland) Regulations 2018, No.370

2. **Best Start foods**
   2 The Welfare Foods (Best Start Foods) (Scotland) Regulations 2019, No.193

3. **Funeral support payments**
   3 The Funeral Expense Assistance (Scotland) Regulations 2019 (draft)

Part 2
Student support

… 15

Chapter 15
Student support

This chapter covers:
1. Full-time higher education (below)
2. Full-time further education (p124)
3. Part-time students (p127)
4. Postgraduates (p128)
5. Nursing and midwifery students (p128)
6. Other support for students (p129)

This chapter outlines the support available for people studying in Scotland who are eligible for student support under the Scottish system. It lists the type of support available, but does not describe the rules for qualifying for it – eg, residence rules. For where to find information on claiming student support and how much you might get, see Appendix 2. See Chapter 16 for how student support affects universal credit, Chapter 17 for how it affects means-tested benefits, Chapter 18 for how it affects tax credits and Chapter 19 for how it affects health benefits.

Basic facts
– Most full-time undergraduate students are eligible for a student loan, and may also get a bursary and living costs grant.
– Full-time students in non-advanced education may be eligible for a bursary maintenance allowance, and grants for travel and study costs.
– Part-time students may get help with fees and other limited support.

1. Full-time higher education

This section is for full-time undergraduates (including allied healthcare students) and full-time students on Higher National Certificate (HNC)/Higher National Diploma (HND) courses. It is also relevant for full-time students on Professional Graduate Diploma in Education courses. Funding is different for other full-time postgraduates (see p128) and for nursing and midwifery students (see p128).

121

Chapter 15: Student support
1. Full-time higher education

Student support from the Student Awards Agency Scotland (SAAS) is made up of:[1]
- tuition fees;
- student loan;
- care experienced students' bursary;
- young students' bursary;
- independent students' bursary;
- dependants' grant;
- lone parents' grant;
- care experienced accommodation grant;
- disabled students' allowance.

In addition, your college or university administers a:
- lone parents' childcare grant;
- discretionary fund;
- childcare fund.

Travel expenses are no longer available, except for students doing a compulsory year abroad, for a placement on an allied health professions or nursing course, and for disabled students who cannot use public transport.

Previous study

You cannot usually get your tuition fees paid if you have previously been on a full-time higher education course and had help from public funds. You may, however, get one year's additional funding if you need this – eg, to change courses or repeat a period of study. This is known as a 'plus one' year.

Contact SAAS to check your entitlement. Even if you are not entitled to help with your tuition fees, you can normally apply for a student loan and living costs grants.

Tuition fees

Tuition fees are paid directly to your college or university. Your income is not assessed and the amounts are not repayable. If your fees are higher than the amounts payable, you must pay the difference.

Tuition fees 2019/20

HNC/HND or equivalent	£1,285
Degree or equivalent	£1,820

Student loan

Student loans are low-interest loans for students, only repayable when you have graduated and are earning over £18,330 a year. You repay the loan at a rate of

9 per cent of your income which exceeds £18,330. Student loans are partly based on your income. You must provide a national insurance number in order to get a loan. If you do not have one, you can apply to the DWP.[2]

Maximum student loan 2019/20

Family income	Dependent student under 25	Independent student under 25, or student aged 25 or over
Below £24,000	£5,750	£6,750
£24,000 to £33,999	£5,750	£6,250
£34,000 or over	£4,750	£4,750

Care experienced students' bursary

Students who have previously been looked after by a local authority in the UK and who are under 26 at the start of their course are eligible for a care experienced students' bursary.[3] This is a non-income-assessed grant of £8,100 in 2019/20, and is paid instead of the student loan/bursary package.

Young students' bursary

You are eligible for a young students' bursary if you are under 25 on the first day of the first academic year of your course (for an autumn start course, this is 1 August) and from a family with an income of less than £34,000 a year. The amount of the bursary depends on your and your family's income. In 2019/20, a maximum of £2,000 is paid if your and your family's combined income is under £21,000 a year. It is paid on top of the maximum loan of £5,750.

Independent students' bursary

The independent students' bursary is paid in addition to the maximum loan of £6,750. Students classed as independent are eligible for £1,000 if their household income is below £21,000 a year.

Dependants' grant

A dependants' grant is an income-assessed, non-repayable grant that you can claim for a spouse, civil partner, partner, or adult dependant who you care for. The maximum amount in 2019/20 is £2,640. The maximum amount is paid if the adult dependant's income is under £1,160 per year.

Lone parents' grant

If you are a lone parent, you can get a lone parents' grant, worth £1,305 in 2019/20, if you have at least one dependent child. Your income is assessed and the grant is not repayable.

Care experienced accommodation grant

If you were in local authority care and are under 26 at the start of your course, you may get a grant of up to £105 (2019/20) a week to help with your accommodation costs during the long vacation. Your income is not assessed and the grant is not repayable.

Disabled students' allowance

If you have a disability or learning difficulty, you can claim for extra expenses that arise because you are on the course. Your income is not assessed and the allowance is not repayable. You can also apply for travel costs if you cannot use public transport because of your disability.

Disabled students' allowance 2019/20

Non-medical personal help	£20,520
Other qualifying costs	£1,725
Specialist equipment (amount per course)	£5,160

Lone parents' childcare grant

If you are a lone parent who receives a lone parents' grant, you can also get a childcare grant to help with the cost of registered or formal childcare. If you are eligible, you are guaranteed up to £1,215 in 2019/20, depending on your actual childcare costs. Your income is not assessed and the grant is not repayable. It is administered by colleges and universities.

Childcare fund

The discretionary childcare fund helps with the cost of registered or formal childcare. It is administered by colleges and universities. They decide who is eligible and how much you can get.

Discretionary funds

Colleges and universities administer discretionary funds to help with living costs, and decide how much the payments will be. You are expected to apply for a full student loan before asking for help. The maximum available is £4,000 in 2019/20.

2. Full-time further education

The Scottish Funding Council gives money to colleges to provide support for further education (FE) students. Colleges must follow national guidelines in allocating their funds.

The following allowances are available to students attending college on a full-time course:[4]
- education maintenance allowance;
- bursary maintenance allowance;
- care experienced students' bursary;
- dependants' allowance;
- additional support needs for learning allowance;
- study expenses allowance;
- travel expenses allowance.

In addition, the following funds are available:[5]
- FE discretionary fund;
- childcare fund;
- lone parents' childcare grant.

Education maintenance allowance

An education maintenance allowance is a means-tested weekly allowance for 16–19-year-olds, paid fortnightly in arrears during term time, but not during breaks.

You can claim from the autumn term if your 16th birthday falls between 1 March 2019 and 30 September 2019. You can claim from the winter term if your 16th birthday falls between 1 October 2019 and 29 February 2020. If you had an allowance previously, you can claim again if you are continuing in further education for up to three years (four years if you are regarded as 'vulnerable'). If you can get an education maintenance allowance, you cannot usually get a bursary maintenance allowance as well, unless you live away from your parents' home (see below).

You get an education maintenance allowance of £30 a week if your household income is £24,421 or less (£26,884 if your parents have another child under 16, or under 25 in education).

Bursary maintenance allowance

The bursary maintenance allowance is an income-assessed allowance and is discretionary. It is not repayable.

Maximum weekly maintenance allowance 2019/20

	Parental home	Elsewhere
Receiving education maintenance allowance	–	£41.60
Receiving universal credit (UC)	£28.00	£28.00
18 to 24	£82.81	£104.65
25 or over	£104.65	£104.65

Chapter 15: Student support
2. Full-time further education

Students entitled to an education maintenance allowance and living away from home or whose parental home is not within reasonable travelling distance of the college may be able to get an allowance of £41.60 a week. Other students getting an education maintenance allowance are not eligible for a bursary maintenance allowance.

Students aged 18 to 24 who are self-supporting, or whose parental home is not within reasonable travelling distance of the college, may be able to get an allowance of £104.65. Otherwise, they may be able to get £82.81.

The bursary is different if you have been in local authority care (see below).

A student who gets UC may be eligible for a weekly bursary of £28.

You may be able to get a bursary to pay up to £116.79 a week rent for college accommodation or college-approved lodgings. Instead of the standard maintenance allowance, you get a personal allowance of £30.59 a week. If you get an education maintenance allowance, you can also get your college accommodation rent paid in this way but do not get the extra personal allowance in addition to this.

Care experienced students' bursary

A care-experienced students' bursary is an award of bursary maintenance allowance paid to a student who has been in local authority care. It is £202.50 a week from age 16 (sometimes 15) onwards. To qualify, you must be under 26 on the first day of the academic year in which your course starts (usually 1 August).

Dependants' allowance

You can claim an allowance of £56.31 a week for a dependent adult for whom you have care, or financial or legal responsibilities, and whose weekly income is less than £56.31.

Additional support needs for learning allowance

You may be able to get support towards study and travel expenses if you have extra expenses because of a disability. The amounts are at the discretion of the college. You can get this allowance in addition to an education maintenance allowance.

Study expenses allowance

The income-assessed study expenses allowance is for items such as books and special clothing. You can get this allowance in addition to an education maintenance allowance.

Travel expenses allowance

You can claim expenses if you have to travel more than two miles (it may be further for some colleges) from your term-time address. You may be able to get travel to college, to a childcare provider, to a mandatory placement and up to eight single journeys between your permanent home and your term-time address. The allowance is income assessed. You can get this allowance in addition to an education maintenance allowance.

Lone parents' childcare grant
If you are an eligible lone parent student, you can get a childcare grant to help with the cost of registered or formal childcare costs. Depending on the costs of childcare, the maximum amount is £1,215 in 2019/20. Your income is not assessed and the grant is not repayable.

Further education discretionary fund
The maximum available from the further education discretionary fund in 2019/20 is £4,000.

Childcare fund
Your college decides how much you can get from the childcare fund.

3. Part-time students

Higher education courses
Part-time students with annual earnings of £25,000 or less can apply for a part-time fee grant. Your course must be between levels seven and 10 of the Scottish Credit and Qualifications Framework and be between 30 and 119 credits a year.

Application forms are available from the Student Awards Agency Scotland (see Appendix 2).

You can also claim a disabled students' allowance (see p124). There is a discretionary fund for part-time students to which you can apply if you are in hardship.

Further education courses

If you are a further education (FE) student studying part time, you can claim some of the same support as full-time students. You can claim:
- support from the childcare fund;
- support from the FE discretionary fund;
- additional support needs for learning allowance;
- study expenses allowance;
- travel expenses allowance.

Your college may be able to waive your fees if you get certain benefits, or have a low income. The education maintenance allowance of £30 per week is available to part-time students as well as full-time students.[6]

4. Postgraduates

The Student Awards Agency Scotland (SAAS) provides support for taught or research-based postgraduate courses at diploma or masters level. The funding is also available for taught or research-based distance-learning postgraduate courses. Awards from SAAS consist of:[7]
- a tuition fee loan of up to £5,500;
- a living-cost loan of up to £4,500 (full-time courses only);
- disabled students' allowance.

Part-time postgraduate students can apply for the tuition fee loan of £5,500.

All postgraduate students can also apply to the postgraduate discretionary fund and childcare fund.

Research councils also give awards for postgraduate courses and each have their own rules for how grants are awarded. Typically, an award may consist of tuition fees, a maintenance grant, dependants' grant, disabled students' allowance and a research support grant.

Social work students can apply to the Scottish Social Services Council for a postgraduate bursary made up of an income-assessed grant, supplementary grants, travel costs for placements and tuition fees.

Professional Graduate Diploma in Education students are eligible for the same support as undergraduates (see p121).

Self-funding full- and part-time postgraduates can get a disabled students' allowance from SAAS.

5. Nursing and midwifery students

Nursing and midwifery students may be able to get a bursary and grants for living costs. Application forms are available from the Student Awards Agency Scotland (see Appendix 2).

A nursing and midwifery discretionary fund is also available.

Bursary

If you are a nursing or midwifery diploma or degree student starting your course in autumn 2019, you can get a non-means-tested nursing and midwifery bursary of £8,100. In the first year, an extra £60 initial expenses allowance is paid. In the fourth year, the bursary is reduced to 75 per cent.

Grants for living costs

The following grants are available for your living costs:
- means-tested dependants' allowance for a spouse, civil partner, partner or dependent child(ren). The allowance is £3,640 for an adult or first child, and

£557 for each subsequent child. **Note:** support for children is still included in nursing and midwifery bursaries, even though it has been abolished for other undergraduates;
- single parents' allowance of £2,303 if you are single, widowed, divorced or separated and bringing up children on your own;
- childcare allowance of up to £2,466 if you pay for registered or formal childcare;
- disabled students' allowance (see p124);
- travel expenses and 'reasonable accommodation costs' for placements.

6. Other support for students

Sponsorship and scholarships
Some companies and government departments sponsor students on their courses.

Educational trusts and endowments
Some charitable trusts provide funds, usually small amounts, to students. For example, Family Action has an educational grants programme (www.family-action.org.uk/what-we-do/grants/educational-grants). The Student Awards Agency Scotland has a register of education endowments at www.saas.gov.uk/_forms/ree1.pdf, which lists Scottish trusts that may be able to help. Lead Scotland also has a list of trusts that provide educational grants at www.lead.org.uk/charitable-trusts-providing-educational-grants-for-individuals. Otherwise, check your local library for information.

SDS Individual Training Accounts
You can get £200 a year towards course fees from an approved learning provider. You can only do one course a year, which must be to help you get a job or progress in your career. See Appendix 2 for contact details.

Chapter 15: Student support
Notes

Notes

1. Full-time higher education
1. **Loans** The Education (Student Loans) (Scotland) Regulations 2007, No.154
   Grants The Students' Allowances (Scotland) Regulations 2007, No.153
   See also Student Awards Agency Scotland, *Guide to Undergraduate Funding 2019-2020* at www.saas.gov.uk/_forms/sas9.pdf
2. The Social Security (National Insurance Numbers) Amendment Regulations 2006, No.2897
3. www.saas.gov.uk/_forms/care_experienced_students.pdf

2. Full-time further education
4. Scottish Funding Council, *National Policy for Further Education Bursaries: 2019-20*, May 2019; Scottish Funding Council, *Education Maintenance Allowance AY 2019-20*, July 2019
5. Scottish Funding Council, *2019-20 National Policy: further education discretionary fund*, May 2019; Scottish Funding Council, *2019-20 National Policy: childcare funds for further and higher education students in Scotland's colleges*, June 2019

3. Part-time students
6. Scottish Funding Council, *Education Maintenance Allowance AY 2019-20*, July 2019

4. Postgraduates
7. Student Awards Agency Scotland, *Guide to Postgraduate Funding 2019-2020* at www.saas.gov.uk/_forms/sas9.pdf

Part 3
Treatment of income

Chapter 16
How income affects universal credit

This chapter covers:
1. Working out your income (below)
2. Grants and loans (p134)
3. Dividing income throughout the year (p136)
4. Other payments (p137)
5. Earnings (p137)
6. Benefits (p138)
7. Maintenance (p138)
8. Savings and other capital (p138)

This chapter explains how much weekly income is taken into account when working out your entitlement to universal credit (UC). If you are claiming income support, income-based jobseeker's allowance, income-related employment and support allowance or housing benefit, see Chapter 17. If you are claiming child tax credit or working tax credit, see Chapter 18.

> **Basic facts**
> – Student loans and some grants count as income when working out how much universal credit you can get.
> – Loans and grants are taken into account as income during the academic year, but ignored in the summer vacation.
> – The maximum amount of student loan to which you are entitled is taken into account as income, whether or not you apply for it.

1. Working out your income

If you have student income (a student loan and grants paid to you for your course), it usually counts as income for universal credit (UC).[1] This chapter explains how much monthly income counts in the assessment.

Chapter 16: How income affects universal credit
2. Grants and loans

Step one	Add together the annual income from grants and loan.
	Add the annual amount of any grants, ignoring those that are disregarded, to the annual amount of any loan (see below).
Step two	Work out the period over which your student income counts.
	Calculate this from the month in which you start your course until the month before the summer vacation, or end of your course, as applicable (see p136).
Step three	Divide income throughout the year.
	Divide the amount in Step one by the number of months over which your student income counts for that year (see p136).
Step four	Deduct disregard.
	Deduct a set amount of £110 from the monthly amount of income from grants and loan.
Step five	Add other income to the monthly amount.
	Add any other income taken into account (eg, earnings) to the monthly amount of your grant and loan (see p137). This, added to the total at Step four, is the amount of income used in the UC assessment.

2. Grants and loans

If you get a student loan

If you are eligible for a loan for maintenance, it counts as income when working out universal credit (UC). The maximum loan you could be entitled to is taken into account, as though there were no reduction for household income or another grant.[2]

Any other grants you receive are disregarded, except for any amount for the maintenance of your partner and/or child(ren), and any specific amount for rent payments that are met by UC.[3] A dependants' grant or lone parents' grant paid as well as your loan counts as income. A discretionary fund payment is ignored, provided it is not for the maintenance of your partner or child(ren), and not a specified amount for rent that is met by UC.

Taken into account	Ignored
Postgraduate loan for living costs	Postgraduate tuition fee loan
Undergraduate loan	Independent students' bursary
Young students' bursary	Tuition fees
Dependants' grant	Disabled students' allowance
Lone parents' grant	Travel expenses
	Lone parents' childcare grant and childcare fund payments

If you do not get a student loan

If you do not get a loan, but you receive a grant, the grant income is taken into account for UC (subject to the disregards below).[4] A grant is an educational grant or award, and does not include education maintenance allowance payments.[5]

Grant income is completely disregarded if you do not get a loan and the grant is paid for:[6]
- tuition fees or exams;
- your disability;
- extra costs of residential study away from your usual place of study during term time;
- the costs of your normal home (if you live elsewhere during your course), unless these are included in your UC;
- the maintenance of someone not included in your UC claim;
- books, equipment, course travel costs or childcare costs.

If you get a grant but no loan and receive a discretionary fund payment, this is disregarded if it is paid for any of the above, and otherwise counts as income.

Taken into account	Ignored
All students	Help with tuition fees
Undergraduate students	
Care experienced students' bursary	
Care experienced accommodation grant	
Nursing and midwifery students	
Nursing and midwifery bursary	Childcare allowance
Dependants' allowance for adult and child	Disabled students' allowance
Single parents' allowance	
Further education students	
Bursary maintenance allowance	Education maintenance allowance
Dependants' allowance	Additional support needs for learning allowance
Care experienced students' bursary	Study and travel expenses allowance
	Lone parents' childcare grant and childcare fund payments

Chapter 16: How income affects universal credit
3. Dividing income throughout the year

3. Dividing income throughout the year

Universal credit (UC) is paid monthly, for an 'assessment period'. Each assessment period runs from the day of the month you claimed UC, for one month – eg, if you claim on the second of the month, each assessment period runs from the second of the month to the first of the following month. The annual amount of your student income must be divided over the number of assessment periods in the course year to arrive at the monthly amount that is used to work out UC.

Student income counts for each assessment period during your course, excluding the one at the end of each academic year and those in the long vacation.[7]

Student income counts as income:
- from the start of the assessment period in which the course/course year begins; *and*
- for every subsequent assessment period during the course/course year.

Student income is ignored:[8]
- in the assessment period in which the last week of the course or the start of the long vacation falls;
- in any assessment period that falls completely within the long vacation; *and*
- if you abandon or leave your course completely, in the assessment period in which you leave.

Long vacation
The **'long vacation'** is the longest holiday in a course which lasts at least two years, and must last for at least one month.[9]

Once you have calculated the number of assessment periods in the course year, divide the total annual amount of loans and/or grants by this number, and apply the monthly disregard. One hundred and ten pounds of student income is disregarded in each assessment period.[10]

Examples
Laura has a five-year-old daughter and is single. She starts a degree course. Year one of her course runs from 30 September 2019 to 15 May 2020. Her assessment periods run from the third of the month to the second of the following month.

Step one   Laura gets a loan of £6,750, independent students' bursary of £1,000 and lone parents' grant of £1,305.

Step two   Her independent students' bursary is disregarded. Her loan and lone parents' grant (total £8,055) count as income over eight assessment periods in the first year of her course (from 3 September 2019 to 2 May 2020).

Step three	£8,055 ÷ 8 = £1,006.88
Step four	£1,006.88 – £110 = £896.88
Step five	She has no other income. Laura's UC is calculated on student income of £896.88 a month from 3 September 2019 to 2 May 2020. From 3 May 2020, weekly income from her student funding is nil. Laura's next UC payment in June 2020 will be based on £0 student funding.

Paula has a seven-year-old son and is single. Her course runs from 2 September 2019 to 5 June 2020. Her assessment periods run from the 14th of the month to the 13th of the following month.

Step one	Paula gets a further education bursary maintenance allowance of £1,120 (40 weeks at £28).
Step two	Her bursary counts as income over nine assessment periods (from 14 August 2019 to 13 May 2020).
Step three	£1,120 ÷ 9 = £124.44
Step four	£124.44 – £110 = £14.44
Step five	She has no other income. Paula's UC is calculated on student income of £14.44 a month from 14 August 2019 to 13 May 2020.

4. Other payments

Professional and career development loans
Professional and career development loans count as capital if paid as a lump sum. If paid in instalments, they normally also count as capital.[11]

SDS Individual Training Account payments
The £200 payment is disregarded.[12]

5. Earnings

Your earnings and your partner's earnings are taken into account in the universal credit (UC) assessment. Your net monthly earnings are taken into account – ie, after deducting:
- income tax;
- class 1 national insurance contributions; *and*
- any contribution you make towards a personal or occupational pension.

Some of your earnings are disregarded if you have children or if you are ill or disabled. This is known as a 'work allowance'. The lower work allowance if you get help with housing costs (rent or service charges) in your UC is £287 a month.

Chapter 16: How income affects universal credit
8. Savings and other capital

You get a higher work allowance of £503 if you have no help with housing costs in your UC. Earnings above your work allowance are deducted at 63 pence for every pound above the allowance. If you do not get a work allowance, 63 pence for every pound of your earnings is deducted from your UC amount.

For full details of the way earnings are treated, see CPAG's *Welfare Benefits and Tax Credits Handbook*.

6. Benefits

Some benefits are taken into account in the assessment of your universal credit, and others are ignored.

Benefits taken into account include:
- carer's allowance;
- contribution-based jobseeker's allowance;
- contributory employment and support allowance;
- most industrial injuries benefits;
- maternity allowance;
- retirement pension.

Benefits that are ignored include:
- attendance allowance;
- Best Start grant;
- carer's allowance supplement and young carer grant;
- child benefit;
- disability living allowance;
- funeral support payments;
- personal independence payment.

7. Maintenance

Child maintenance payments are ignored completely for universal credit. Other types of maintenance (eg, money from your former spouse to maintain you) may count as income. For details, see CPAG's *Welfare Benefits and Tax Credits Handbook*.

8. Savings and other capital

There are limits on the amount of savings and other capital you can have and still claim universal credit (UC). Some kinds of capital are not counted in the assessment. For details, see CPAG's *Welfare Benefits and Tax Credits Handbook*.

Chapter 16: How income affects universal credit
Notes

You cannot get UC if your savings or other capital are above £16,000.
If your capital is £6,000 or less, it does not affect your UC at all.
If your capital is between £6,000.01 and £16,000, you are treated as though you have income from this capital of £4.35 a month for every £250 or part of £250 between these limits. For example, if you have savings of £6,525, your assumed income is £13.05 a month.

Notes

1. **Working out your income**
    1 Reg 66(1)(e) UC Regs

2. **Grants and loans**
    2 Regs 68 and 69 UC Regs
    3 Reg 68(3) UC Regs
    4 Reg 68(2) and (4) UC Regs
    5 Reg 68(7) UC Regs
    6 Reg 70 UC Regs

3. **Dividing income throughout the year**
    7 Reg 68 UC Regs
    8 Reg 13 UC Regs
    9 Reg 68(7) UC Regs
    10 Reg 71 UC Regs

4. **Other payments**
    11 Reg 46(4) UC Regs
    12 Reg 70(a) UC Regs

Chapter 17

How income affects means-tested benefits

This chapter covers:
1. Working out your income (p141)
2. Grants and loans (p142)
3. Dividing student income throughout the year (p146)
4. Discretionary funds and other payments (p153)
5. Earnings (p155)
6. Benefits and tax credits (p156)
7. Maintenance (p156)
8. Savings and other capital (p157)

This chapter explains how much weekly income is taken into account when working out your entitlement to income support, income-based jobseeker's allowance, income-related employment and support allowance and housing benefit. For information on how income affects universal credit, see Chapter 16. Although tax credits are also means tested, the way student and other income is assessed is different (see Chapter 18).

> **Basic facts**
> – Student loans are normally divided over 42 or 43 weeks from the beginning of September to the end of June and taken into account as income for means-tested benefits during that period. If your income is too high, you do not get income support, income-based jobseeker's allowance or income-related employment and support allowance, and your housing benefit (HB) is reduced.
> – The amount of student loan you are eligible for is taken into account as income, whether or not you apply for it.
> – If you or your partner are over pension age, your student grant and loan are ignored as income for HB.
> – Student loans are normally *not* taken into account as income for means-tested benefits from around the end of June until the beginning of September. You may be able to get benefit (or more benefit) during these months even if your income was too high during the academic year.
> – Some grants are also taken into account as income, but others do not affect your benefit.

Chapter 17: How income affects means-tested benefits
1. Working out your income

The way that student income is taken into account for income support (IS), income-based jobseeker's allowance, income-related employment and support allowance (ESA) and housing benefit (HB) is essentially the same (see Chapter 16 for universal credit). Chapters 4, 6 and 7 outline the income-related ESA, HB and IS assessments step by step. This chapter explains how much weekly income counts in these assessments.

Step one — **Add together the annual income from grants and loan.**
Add the annual amount of any student grants, ignoring any that are wholly disregarded (see p142), to the annual amount of any student loan. Do not include the care experienced accommodation grant, which is paid for the long vacation only.

Step two — **Apply annual disregards.**
From the total annual grants and loan, deduct any disregarded amounts for books and equipment, and for travel (see p142).

Step three — **Divide income into a weekly amount.**
Divide the annual amount of grants and loan by the number of benefit weeks in the period over which your grants and loan are counted as income for benefit purposes (see p146).

Step four — **Deduct any weekly disregard.**
If you have a student loan, deduct £10 – this is the weekly disregard.

Step five — **Add other income to the weekly amount.**
Add together any other weekly income (eg, from discretionary funds or a professional and career development loan), earnings (p155), tariff income from capital (p157), and benefits and tax credits (p156). Ignore any amount that is disregarded. This total, added to the weekly grants and loan total at Step four, is the amount of income used in the benefit assessment.

If you want to work out your benefit entitlement during the long vacation, p146 explains when the long vacation starts and finishes for benefit purposes – ie, when your student loan or grant counts as nil income. You should then total on a weekly basis any other income you have over the vacation (including a care experienced accommodation grant if you have one).

Chapter 17: How income affects means-tested benefits
2. Grants and loans

2. Grants and loans

Grants

A grant is defined as an educational grant or award, bursary, scholarship or allowance, and does not include education maintenance allowance or discretionary fund payments.[1] In general, grants intended for living costs are taken into account and grants for other costs are disregarded. For the way that discretionary funds are treated, see p153.

If you are *not* eligible for a student loan, deduct from your grant:
- £390 for books and equipment;
- £303 for travel.

An assessed contribution from a partner or parent counts as income, whether or not you receive it. However, for income support (IS) and income-related employment and support allowance (ESA), if you are a disabled student, only include contributions that are actually paid.[2]

Ignore any grants for:[3]
- tuition fees or exam fees;
- course-related disability costs;
- residential study away from your normal home;
- books and equipment, or travel;
- for IS, income-based jobseeker's allowance (JSA) and income-related ESA only, maintenance of a child dependant;
- childcare costs.

Undergraduate grants

The following higher education (HE) grants are disregarded:
- lone parents' childcare grant;[4]
- disabled students' allowance;[5]
- lone parents' grant for income-related ESA, and for IS and income-based JSA except for some existing claimants who do not get child tax credit (CTC) (see p143);
- travel expenses;[6]
- tuition fees.[7]

The following HE grants are taken into account:
- young students' bursary;
- independent students' bursary;
- care experienced students' bursary;
- care experienced accommodation grant;

- dependants' grant;
- lone parents' grant. This is always taken into account for housing benefit (HB), but disregarded for IS, income-based JSA and income-related ESA.[8]

Nursing and midwifery students' grants

The following grants are disregarded:
- childcare allowance;
- disabled students' allowance;
- dependants' allowance for a child, and single parents' allowance – for IS, income-based JSA and income-related ESA.

The following are taken into account:
- nursing and midwifery bursary;
- single parents' allowance – for HB;
- dependants' allowance for an adult;
- dependants' allowance for a child – for HB.

Postgraduate grants

The following are taken into account:
- maintenance grant;
- dependants' grant.

Grants in further education

The following further education (FE) grants are disregarded:
- education maintenance allowance;[9]
- additional support needs for learning allowance for disability costs;[10]
- study expenses allowance if paid for books and equipment;[11]
- lone parents' childcare grant;[12]
- travel expenses allowance.[13]

The following FE grants are taken into account:
- bursary maintenance allowance;
- care experienced students' bursary;
- dependants' allowance.

FE students who are lone parents and other students eligible for IS (see p56) or income-related ESA can stay on IS or income-related ESA instead of applying for a discretionary bursary maintenance allowance. This is because the rules can only treat you as having access to such income if it 'would become available to [you] upon application'.[14] You should not be treated as having access to a discretionary bursary if you do not have one because, by its nature, there is no guarantee you would get it if you applied.

Chapter 17: How income affects means-tested benefits
2. Grants and loans

Grants and loans checklist

Student support	Treatment
Undergraduate income	
Student loan (including young students' bursary)	Disregard: – £390 a year for books and equipment; – £303 a year for travel; – £10 a week; – amount of student's contribution to loan; – partner's contribution.
Independent students' bursary	Taken into account in full.
Care experienced students' bursary	Disregard: – £390 a year for books and equipment; – £303 a year for travel.
Care experienced accommodation grant	Taken into account in full.
Dependants' grant	Taken into account in full.
Disabled students' allowance	Disregarded.
Lone parents' grant	Taken into account in full for HB. Disregarded for IS and income-based JSA if you get CTC. Disregarded for income-related ESA.
Lone parents' childcare grant	Disregarded.
Travel expenses	Disregarded.
Discretionary funds	Taken into account if paid for basic living costs (as capital if not regular payments) less a weekly disregard. Disregarded if paid for other items.
Childcare fund	Disregarded.
Part-time fee grant	Disregarded.
Nursing and midwifery student income	
Nursing and midwifery bursary	Disregard: – £390 a year for books and equipment; – £303 a year for travel.
Dependants' allowance for adult	Taken into account in full.
Dependants' allowance for child	Taken into account in full for HB. Disregarded for IS and income-based JSA if you get CTC. Disregarded for income-related ESA.
Single parents' allowance	Taken into account in full for HB. Disregarded for IS and income-based JSA if you get CTC. Disregarded for income-related ESA.

Chapter 17: How income affects means-tested benefits
2. Grants and loans

Childcare allowance	Disregarded.
Disabled students' allowance	Disregarded.

Postgraduate income

Tuition fees (including tuition fee loan) and exam fees	Disregarded.
Postgraduate living cost loan	Disregard: – £390 a year for books and equipment; – £303 a year for travel.
Residential study	Disregarded.
Books, equipment and travel	Disregarded.
Maintenance grant	Disregard: – £390 a year for books and equipment; – £303 a year for travel.

Further education income

Bursary maintenance allowance	Disregard: – £390 a year for books and equipment; – £303 a year for travel.
Care experienced students' bursary	Disregard: – £390 a year for books and equipment; – £303 a year for travel.
Dependants' allowance	Taken into account in full.
Education maintenance allowance	Disregarded.
Additional support needs for learning allowance	Disregarded for disability costs.
Study expenses allowance	Disregarded for books and equipment.
Lone parents' childcare grant	Disregarded.
Travel expenses allowance	Disregarded.
Childcare fund	Disregarded.
FE discretionary fund	Taken into account less weekly disregard if paid for basic living costs. Disregarded if paid for other items.

Student loan

You should include in the student loan:
- the maximum loan for which you are eligible, including the young students' bursary.[15] This is taken into account as your income whether or not you apply for it.[16] This means that students cannot choose to keep maximum IS or income-related ESA instead of applying for a loan; you are treated as though you had taken out the full loan and your benefit reduced accordingly;

Chapter 17: How income affects means-tested benefits
3. Dividing student income throughout the year

- the assessed contribution from a parent or partner, whether or not you receive it. However, for IS and income-related ESA, if you are a disabled student, only contributions that are actually paid are included.[17]

You should deduct from the annual student loan:
- £390 for books and equipment;
- £303 for travel.

There is a further disregard of £10 a week that applies once the student loan has been divided over the number of weeks in the period of study to arrive at a weekly amount.[18]

3. Dividing student income throughout the year

The annual amount of your loan and grant must be divided over the number of weeks in, usually, a standard academic year to arrive at the weekly amount used to calculate income support (IS), income-based jobseeker's allowance (JSA), income-related employment and support allowance (ESA) and housing benefit (HB). The **'standard academic year'** begins on 1 September, 1 January, 1 April or 1 July depending on whether your course begins in the autumn, winter, spring or summer.[19] Courses that start in August are taken to have an academic year starting on 1 September.[20] Rules specify exactly the weeks over which the loan and grant are taken into account.

Student loans

Student loans are normally divided over 42 or 43 weeks from the beginning of September to the end of June. During this period, your student loan is taken into account as your income in the assessment of IS, income-based JSA, income-related ESA and HB. If your income is too high, you are not eligible for these benefits. However, your student loan is not taken into account from around the end of June to the beginning of September. Because your income goes down in these months (unless you have other income – eg, from earnings), you may be able to get benefit during the summer. It is important, therefore, to make a claim from the end of June, even if you were refused benefit at the start of the academic year.

The details of the weeks over which your loan is taken into account are as follows.

Courses starting in the autumn term lasting more than a year

The student loan is divided over the number of weeks starting from the first day of the first benefit week in September until the last day of the last benefit week in June.[21] In 2019/20 this is 42 weeks for benefit weeks that begin on a Thursday,

Chapter 17: How income affects means-tested benefits
3. Dividing student income throughout the year

Friday or Saturday and 43 weeks for benefit weeks that begin on a Monday, Tuesday or Wednesday. If your course starts in August, you count the weeks starting from the first day of the first benefit week on or after the start of your course, until the last day of the last benefit week in June.

This is the period over which your loan is taken into account as income in the benefit assessment, unless you do not count as a student at all. For example, at the start of your first year, you do not count as being a student until you actually start attending or undertaking the course. In other words, in the first year the loan is still divided over 42/43 weeks, but the weekly amount arrived at is ignored as income until you start your course.[22]

In the final year of study, the loan is divided over the number of benefit weeks starting from the first day of the first benefit week in September (or the start of the first term if it starts in August) until the end of the benefit week on or before the last day of the final academic term.[23]

For HB, the start of the benefit week is a Monday.[24] For IS, JSA and ESA, it depends on your national insurance (NI) number.[25]

Example: first-year student claiming income support
Samira is in her first year. She has two children aged three and 10 and gets child tax credit (CTC) for them. She gets a student loan of £6,750, an independent students' bursary of £1,000 and a lone parents' grant of £1,305. Her first term begins on Monday 23 September 2019. Her benefit weeks start on Thursdays. Her student loan is divided over the weeks from Thursday 5 September 2019 until Wednesday 24 June 2020 (42 weeks) to get a weekly income figure. However, because she is in her first year, she does not count as a student until she starts university on 23 September and so her student income is ignored until then. Because she gets CTC, the lone parents' grant is ignored for IS.

From the start of term:
Her weekly loan and grant income is:

	£
Loan plus independent students' bursary	7,750
Less disregards for books and equipment (£390) and travel (£303)	7,057
Divided by 42 weeks =	168.02
Less £10 weekly loan disregard =	158.02

£158.02 is taken into account as weekly income from her loan and grants between Thursday 26 September 2019 and 24 June 2020.
Her IS applicable amount is £73.10 a week. She gets her usual IS up until she starts her course. From 26 September, her IS stops because her income is higher than her IS applicable amount.

At the end of the academic year:
Her weekly income from her loan between 25 June and 2 September 2020 is nil. Samira cannot reclaim IS, but would be eligible for universal credit (UC). She should get a better-off calculation to check whether she should claim UC or remain on CTC.

Chapter 17: How income affects means-tested benefits
3. Dividing student income throughout the year

Example: second-year student claiming housing benefit
Agnes is in her second year. She has one child aged two and is claiming HB as a lone parent. She gets a student loan and an independent students' bursary which total £7,750. She also gets a lone parents' grant of £1,305. Her first term begins on 9 September 2019. Her student loan is divided over the weeks from Monday 2 September 2019 until Sunday 28 June 2020 (43 weeks).
The weekly loan income taken into account is:

	£
Loan plus grants	9,055
Less disregards for books and equipment (£390) and travel (£303)	8,362
Divided by 43 weeks =	194.47
Less £10 weekly loan disregard =	184.47

£184.47 is taken into account as weekly income from her loan between 2 September 2019 and 28 June 2020. Her weekly income from her loan between 29 June and 6 September 2020 is nil.

Courses not starting in the autumn term
Your student loan is divided over the number of weeks starting from the first day of the first benefit week on or after the beginning of a standard academic year (see p146), and ending on the last day of the last benefit week on or before the last day of the academic year, but excluding benefit weeks that fall entirely within the quarter that is taken by the DWP to be the longest vacation.[26]

Academic years and quarters
'**Academic years**' in this case are 12 months, beginning on 1 January, 1 April or 1 July for courses that begin in winter, spring or summer respectively.
'**Quarters**' are 1 January to 31 March, 1 April to 30 June, 1 July to 31 August, 1 September to 31 December.[27]

Example
Anya's course begins on 6 January 2020. The main vacation is 8 June to 28 August 2020. She is claiming HB and the benefit week starts on a Monday. Her loan is divided over the weeks from Monday 6 January 2020 to Sunday 5 July 2020, and from Monday 31 August 2020 until Sunday 27 December 2020. From 6 July to 30 August 2020, her student loan income is nil for benefit purposes.

Courses lasting one year or less
Your loan is divided over the number of weeks from the first day of the first benefit week on or after the start of a standard academic year (see p146) (or, if a course

Chapter 17: How income affects means-tested benefits
3. Dividing student income throughout the year

begins in August, from the first day of the first benefit week on or after the first day of the course) until the last day of the last benefit week on or before the last day of the course. The weekly amount that results is then taken into account from the point you actually start attending or undertaking the course.[28]

If you leave your course early

If you abandon your course early or are dismissed from it before you have had the final instalment of your student loan in that academic year, the loan continues to be taken into account up until the day before you would have been due your next loan payment, or to the end of the quarter (see p148) in which you left, whichever is earlier. This means that if your loan payments stop shortly after you leave the course, they are only taken into account (and affect any benefits) for a short period.

To calculate the amount of loan taken into account, start by working out the weekly amount of annual loan, with disregards for books, equipment and travel but without the £10 weekly disregard. Then, subtract this amount of weekly loan for the period from the start of the standard academic year (see p146) to the day you left from the amount of loan (minus the £693 disregards) you have been paid so far. The result is then divided over the weeks from when you left to when your next instalment would have been due, or the end of the quarter, whichever is earlier.

Example: income support, jobseeker's allowance and employment and support allowance

Nick abandons his course on 11 October 2019. He is in the second year of a three-year course. He gets a small amount of ESA during his course (which includes a severe disability premium). His benefit week starts on a Monday. In Nick's case, he has already been paid £2,325 of his £7,750 loan/bursary by the date he leaves.

Step one: work out weekly amount of annual loan

	£
Loan/bursary	7,750
Less disregards (£693) =	7,057
Divided by 43 weeks =	164.12

Step two: work out amount of annual loan before leaving the course
Multiply the weekly annual loan by the number of benefit weeks from the week after the one that includes the start of the standard academic year until the week before the one that includes the day Nick left the course.
£164.12 x 5 weeks (2 September to 6 October) = £820.60

Step three: work out amount of loan 'left over' since leaving the course
To do this, add the monthly loan instalments paid or due before the date Nick left his course, deduct disregards, and deduct the annual loan worked out for the period before leaving.

149

Chapter 17: How income affects means-tested benefits
3. Dividing student income throughout the year

	£
Loan up to when left the course	2,325
Less disregards (£693) =	1,632
Amount of loan paid taken into account =	1,632
Deduct annual loan before leaving (£820.60) =	811.40

Step four: work out weekly amount of 'leftover' loan for the period it is taken into account

Divide the total amount of leftover loan from Step three for the period since leaving the course by the number of weeks from when Nick left to the day before he would have been due his next loan payment, or the end of the quarter in which he left, whichever is earlier. Count from the benefit week that includes the day Nick left the course until the benefit week that includes the day before his next loan instalment would have been due had payments continued, or the benefit week that includes the last day of the last quarter for which an instalment was payable, whichever is earlier. In Nick's case, his next loan instalment would have been due on 7 November, and this is before the end of the quarter (31 December).

£811.40 ÷ 5 (7 October to 10 November 2019) = £162.28

£162.28 a week is taken into account from 7 October 2019 until 10 November 2019.

Example: housing benefit

To work out how much loan to take into account for Nick's HB claim (assuming he is not passported to HB from another means-tested benefit) after he has left his course, the calculation is slightly different to that for IS, income-based JSA and income-related ESA. In Step two above, instead of working out the number of benefit weeks up until the week *before* the one that includes the day Nick left the course, count up until the week that *includes* the one on which he left the course – ie, there is an extra week in this part of the calculation. Bear in mind that benefit weeks for HB always start on a Monday, and this may not be the same for IS, JSA or income-related ESA.

Step one: work out weekly amount of annual loan

	£
Loan/bursary	7,750
Less disregards (£693) =	7,057
Divided by 43 weeks =	164.12

Step two: work out amount of annual loan before leaving the course

Multiply the weekly annual loan by the number of benefit weeks from the week after the one that includes the start of the standard academic year until the week that *includes* the day Nick left the course.

£164.12 x 6 (2 September to 13 October) = £984.72

Step three: work out amount of loan 'left over' since leaving the course

In the same way as in the example for IS/JSA/ESA above.

	£
Loan up to when left the course	2,325
Less disregards (£693) =	1,632
Amount of loan to end of term taken into account =	1,632
Deduct annual loan before leaving, from Step two (£984.72) =	647.28

Step four: work out weekly amount of 'leftover' loan for the period it is taken into account
In the same way as in the example for IS/JSA/ESA above.
£647.28 ÷ 5 (7 October to 10 November 2019) = £129.46
£129.46 a week is taken into account from 7 October until 10 November 2019.

Note: if you repay the loan, it is still taken into account as income, according to the formula above.[29] You could, therefore, be refused IS, income-based JSA or income-related ESA despite having no other money to live on. However, if the Student Loans Company asks you to repay the loan rather than your repaying it voluntarily, DWP guidance tells decision makers to disregard the loan as income from the date of the request.[30]

Grants

To work out the weeks over which your grant is taken into account for means-tested benefits, first check whether there is a specific rule for that type of grant or whether the standard rule applies.

The standard rule for grants

If the standard rule applies, the grant is taken into account from:[31]
- the first day of the first benefit week (see p146) on or after the start of the course in the first or only year; *or*
- the first day of the first benefit week on or after that year's start for your course if this is not your first year;

until:
- the last day of the last benefit week that ends on or before the day before the summer vacation if the course continues after the summer; *or*
- the last day of the last benefit week on or before the last day of the final academic term in the final year or on a course lasting a year or less.

The standard rule applies if your grant income is 'attributable' to those weeks. Even though you may be paid your grant monthly, if your grant has been awarded for the whole academic year or length of study, it should be taken into account in this way. You may need to ask your college for a statement showing your annual grant entitlement. This statement should break down the grant into the different

Chapter 17: How income affects means-tested benefits
3. Dividing student income throughout the year

allowances so that the DWP can apply the correct disregards when working out how much benefit you should get.

If your grant has not been awarded for the whole academic year or length of study, it is taken into account over the period for which it is payable, from the first day of the first benefit week on or after the start of the period for which the grant is payable until the last day of the last benefit week on or before the last day of that period.[32]

Higher education grants

For higher education students, the dependants' grant and lone parents' grant (unless it is disregarded) are taken into account over the same period as the student loan if you have a student loan or you are eligible for one.[33] This is the case even though the Student Awards Agency Scotland guide says that such grants cover 52 weeks.

Nursing and midwifery bursaries

Your bursary, dependants' allowance and single parents' allowance (unless it is disregarded), if assessed for study throughout the calendar year, are taken into account for the number of benefit weeks within the full calendar year. Otherwise, the award is taken into account under the standard rule for grants (see p151).

Further education grants

Your bursary is only taken into account as income during the academic year. This means that if you are refused benefit during the academic year because your income is too high, you may qualify during the summer vacation if your course lasts more than a year.

The bursary maintenance allowance and dependants' allowance are taken into account under the standard rule for grants (see p151).

Example: one-year course
Salome is on a one-year course, starting on 5 August 2019 and running until 29 May 2020. She gets a bursary maintenance allowance of £4,499.95 for the year. She is getting HB, so her benefit week begins on a Monday. Her allowance is taken into account from Monday 5 August 2019 until Sunday 24 May 2020 (42 weeks). The weekly amount taken into account over that period is:

	£
Total grants for the year	4,499.95
Less disregards for books and equipment (£390) and travel (£303)	3,806.95
Divided by 42 weeks =	90.64

£90.64 a week is taken into account as income for HB from 5 August 2019 to 24 May 2020.

Postgraduate funding

A postgraduate award that is assessed for study throughout the calendar year is taken into account for the number of benefit weeks in the full calendar year.[34] Otherwise, the award is taken into account under the standard rule for grants (see p151).

Postgraduate student loans are taken into account under the standard rule for loans (see p146). Students on a Professional Graduate Diploma in Education course may get the same student loan and grants as undergraduates, and these are treated in the same way as undergraduate loans and grants.

If you leave your course early

For IS, income-related ESA and income-based JSA, if you abandon your course or get dismissed from it, your grant continues to be taken into account, calculated as though you were still a student, until the end of term or vacation in which you stop being a full-time student or, if earlier, until you repay the grant or the period for which the grant is payable ends.[35]

For HB, your grant is not taken into account as if you were still a student. Instead, it is taken into account until the grant provider asks you to repay it and, until then, should be calculated over an appropriate period.[36] Arguably, your grant should only be taken into account as income until the end of the period your last instalment was meant to cover.

4. Discretionary funds and other payments

Discretionary funds

Discretionary funds are treated differently from student grants and loans. Discretionary funds include:[37]
- higher education (HE) discretionary fund;
- further education (FE) discretionary fund.

In general, if the payment is for certain living costs, it is taken into account in full if it counts as capital, or with up to a £20 a week disregard if it counts as income. If the payment is for other costs, it is disregarded. Ask your college for a letter saying what the payment is for and how it is paid.

A lump-sum payment counts as capital. Regular payments count as income.
The FE and HE childcare funds are disregarded.

Lump-sum payments

Lump-sum payments are taken into account as capital if they are intended and used for food, ordinary clothing or footwear, household fuel, rent met by housing benefit (HB), housing costs met by income support (IS), income-related

Chapter 17: How income affects means-tested benefits
4. Discretionary funds and other payments

employment and support allowance (ESA) or jobseeker's allowance (JSA), council tax or water charges.[38] Payments for anything else are ignored for up to 52 weeks. Although taken into account as capital, such payments only affect your benefit if they bring your capital above the lower limit (see p157). Payments for school uniforms or sports clothes or sports shoes are ignored, as these do not count as 'ordinary clothing or footwear'.[39] Payments for service charges other than fuel charges that HB does not meet are ignored. Payments for rent in excess of the amount that HB will meet are ignored – eg, if your rent is more than the maximum amount covered by HB (see p43).

Regular payments

Regular payments are taken into account as income if they are intended and used for food, ordinary clothing or footwear, household fuel, rent met by HB, housing costs met by IS, JSA or income-related ESA, and council tax or water charges.[40] However, up to £20 a week is disregarded. You cannot get the £20 disregard in full as well as the full weekly disregards available on a student loan (or on widowed parent's allowance or war pensions). If you get one of these other payments as well as a discretionary payment, your maximum weekly disregard is £20.

For example, if you have a student loan and regular payments from the HE discretionary fund, £10 a week is disregarded from each.

Regular payments intended and used for anything else, such as childcare or travel expenses, are completely disregarded.

Payments before a course starts or before a loan is paid

A payment from the discretionary fund made before the course starts is always ignored as income even if it is for living costs. A payment made before you get the first instalment of your student loan, if it is intended to tide you over until your loan is paid, is ignored as income.

Other payments

Voluntary or charitable payments

Regular voluntary or charitable payments are ignored for IS, JSA, income-related ESA and HB. If paid as a lump sum, the payment is taken into account as capital whatever it is intended for.

Professional and career development loans

Professional and career development loans are always treated as income, not capital, irrespective of how they are paid.[41] The loan is taken into account if it is intended and used for food, ordinary clothing or footwear, household fuel, rent met by HB, housing costs met by IS, income-based JSA or income-related ESA, council tax or water charges.[42] If it is paid for anything else (eg, tuition fees, books or travel), it is ignored. Once the period of education supported by the loan is completed, a loan that was previously taken into account is then disregarded.[43]

SDS Individual Training Account payments
The £200 payment is disregarded.[44]

5. Earnings

Your earnings and your partner's earnings are taken into account in the benefit assessment. Your net weekly earnings are taken into account – ie, after deducting:
- income tax;
- class 1 national insurance contributions;
- half of any contribution you make towards a personal or occupational pension.

Some of your earnings are disregarded. Of the following, the highest disregard(s) that applies in your circumstances is deducted from your earnings:
- £25 for lone parents claiming housing benefit (HB);
- £20 for lone parents claiming income support (IS) or income-based jobseeker's allowance;
- £20 for those who get a disability premium;
- £20 for those who get a work-related activity or support component in their HB applicable amount. For those on HB doing permitted work and getting certain other benefits, the disregard can be higher;
- £20 for income-related employment and support (ESA) claimants. This disregard can be higher for those doing permitted work;
- £20 for those who get a carer premium;
- £20 for part-time firefighters and some other emergency auxiliaries;
- £10 for couples, whether one or both are working;
- £5 for single people.

For example, if you are a lone parent who is also disabled, you have £25 disregarded for HB and £20 for IS.

In some cases, for HB, childcare costs for registered childminders, nurseries and playschemes can be disregarded from earnings. Childcare costs of up to £175 a week for one child or £300 for two or more children are deducted from weekly earnings if you are:
- a lone parent who is working;
- in a couple and both of you are working;
- in a couple, one of you is working and one of you is disabled (eg, gets a disability premium) or is in hospital or prison.

In each case, the work must be for 16 hours or more a week.

For HB, an extra £17.10 is disregarded if you work 16 hours or more and have a child or a disability, or work 30 hours or more and are aged 25 or over (and in some other cases).

Chapter 17: How income affects means-tested benefits
7. Maintenance

For full details of the way earnings are treated, see CPAG's *Welfare Benefits and Tax Credits Handbook*.

6. Benefits and tax credits

Some benefits are taken into account in the assessment of income support (IS), income-based jobseeker's allowance (JSA), income-related employment and support allowance (ESA) and housing benefit (HB). Other benefits are ignored or partially ignored.

Benefits and tax credits taken into account in full include:
- carer's allowance (CA);
- child tax credit (CTC) for HB;
- contribution-based JSA;
- contributory ESA;
- incapacity benefit;
- most industrial injuries benefits;
- retirement pension;
- working tax credit.

Benefits and tax credits completely disregarded include:
- attendance allowance;
- Best Start grant;
- CA supplement and the young carer grant;[45]
- child benefit (but if you still have amounts for children in your IS or JSA, child benefit is taken into account);
- CTC for IS, JSA and income-related ESA;
- disability living allowance;
- personal independence payment;
- funeral support payments.

Benefits and tax credits partly disregarded include widowed parent's allowance – £10 a week is disregarded for IS, JSA and income-related ESA, £15 a week for HB. You do not get this disregard in full if you already have £10 disregarded from a student loan or £20 disregarded from discretionary fund payments.

7. Maintenance

Child maintenance payments are disregarded in full for income support, jobseeker's allowance, income-related employment and support allowance and housing benefit.

8. Savings and other capital

There are limits on the amount of savings and other capital you can have and still claim benefit. These limits are described below. Some kinds of capital are not counted in the assessment. For details, see CPAG's *Welfare Benefits and Tax Credits Handbook*.

You cannot get income support, income-based jobseeker's allowance, income-related employment and support allowance or housing benefit (HB) if your savings or other capital are above £16,000.

If your capital is £6,000 or less, it does not affect your benefit at all.

If your capital is between £6,000.01 and £16,000, you are treated as though you have income from this capital of £1 a week for every £250 or part of £250 between these limits. This is referred to as 'tariff income'. For example, if you have savings of £6,525, your tariff income is £3 a week.

These limits are different if you or your partner are over pension age. All your capital is ignored if you or your partner get pension credit guarantee credit. Otherwise, tariff income of £1 for each £500 or part of £500 between £10,000.01 and £16,000 is taken into account in the assessment of HB.

Notes

2. **Grants and loans**
   1 **IS** Reg 61(1) IS Regs
      JSA Reg 130 JSA Regs
      ESA Reg 131(1) ESA Regs
      HB Reg 53(1) HB Regs
      All Definition of 'grant'
   2 **IS** Reg 61(1) IS Regs
      ESA Reg 131(1) ESA Regs
      HB Reg 53(1) HB Regs
   3 **IS** Reg 62(2) IS Regs
      JSA Reg 131(2) JSA Regs
      ESA Reg 132(2) ESA Regs
      HB Reg 59(2) HB Regs
   4 **IS** Reg 62(2)(j) IS Regs
      ESA Reg 132(2)(i) ESA Regs
      HB Reg 59(2)(h) HB Regs
   5 **IS** Reg 62(2)(c) IS Regs
      ESA Reg 132(2)(b) ESA Regs
      HB Reg 59(2)(b) HB Regs
   6 **IS** Reg 62(2)(h) IS Regs
      ESA Reg 132(2)(g) ESA Regs
      HB Reg 59(2)(g) HB Regs
   7 **IS** Reg 62(2)(a) IS Regs
      ESA Reg 132(2)(a) ESA Regs
      HB Reg 59(2)(a) HB Regs
   8 **IS** Reg 62(2)(i) IS Regs
      JSA Reg 131(2)(h) JSA Regs
      ESA Reg 132(2)(h) ESA Regs
      Note: the rules do not specifically disregard the lone parents' grant but rather disregard 'any payment... intended for the maintenance of a child dependant'. Since the SAAS pays this grant only to students with children for their maintenance, it should be disregarded under this rule for IS, income-based JSA and income-related ESA.

Chapter 17: How income affects means-tested benefits
Notes

9 **IS** Sch 9 para 11 IS Regs
JSA Sch 7 para 12 JSA Regs
ESA Sch 8 para 13 ESA Regs
HB Sch 5 para 11 HB Regs
10 **IS** Reg 62(2)(c) IS Regs
JSA Reg 131(2)(b) JSA Regs
ESA Reg 132(2)(b) ESA Regs
HB Reg 59(2)(b) HB Regs
11 **IS** Reg 62(2)(g) IS Regs
ESA Reg 132(2)(f) ESA Regs
HB Reg 59(2)(f) HB Regs
12 **IS** Reg 62(2)(j) IS Regs
ESA Reg 132(2)(i) ESA Regs
HB Reg 59(2)(h) HB Regs
13 **IS** Reg 62(2)(h) IS Regs
JSA Reg 131(2)(g) JSA Regs
ESA Reg 132(2)(g) ESA Regs
HB Reg 59(2)(g) HB Regs
14 **IS** Reg 42(2) IS Regs
ESA Reg 106(2) ESA Regs
15 **IS** Reg 61(1) IS Regs
ESA Reg 131(1) ESA Regs
HB Reg 53(1) HB Regs
All Definition of 'student loan'
16 **IS** Reg 66A(3) and (4) IS Regs
ESA Reg 137(4) and (5) ESA Regs
HB Reg 64(3) and (4) HB Regs
17 **IS** Reg 66A(4)(a) IS Regs
ESA Reg 137(5)(a) ESA Regs
HB Reg 64(4) HB Regs
18 **IS** Reg 66A(2) IS Regs
ESA Reg 137(3) ESA Regs
HB Reg 64(2) HB Regs

3. Dividing student income throughout the year
19 **IS** Reg 61(1) IS Regs
ESA Reg 131(1) ESA Regs
HB Reg 53(1) HB Regs
20 **IS** Reg 61(1) IS Regs
ESA Reg 131(1) ESA Regs
HB Reg 53(1) HB Regs
All Definition of 'academic year'
21 **IS** Reg 66A(2)(c) IS Regs
ESA Reg 137(3)(e) ESA Regs
HB Reg 64(2)(d) HB Regs
22 CIS/3734/2004
23 **IS** Reg 66A(2)(b) IS Regs
ESA Reg 137(3)(d) ESA Regs
HB Reg 64(2)(c) HB Regs
24 Reg 2 HB Regs
25 **IS** Reg 2(1) IS Regs
JSA Reg 1(3) JSA Regs
ESA Reg 2(1) ESA Regs
26 **IS** Reg 66A(2)(aa) IS Regs
ESA Reg 137(3)(b) ESA Regs
HB Reg 64(2)(b) HB Regs

27 **IS** Reg 66A(2)(aa) IS Regs
ESA Reg 137(3)(c) ESA Regs
HB Reg 64(2)(b) HB Regs
28 **IS** Reg 66A(2)(a) IS Regs
ESA Reg 137(3)(a) ESA Regs
HB Reg 64(2)(a) HB Regs
29 CJSA/549/2003
30 Vol 6, para 30470 DMG
31 **IS** Regs 61, definition of 'period of study', and 62(3) IS Regs
ESA Regs 131(1), definition of 'period of study', and 132(4) ESA Regs
HB Regs 53, definition of 'period of study', and 59(5) HB Regs
32 **IS** Reg 62(3)(b) IS Regs
ESA Reg 132(4)(b) ESA Regs
HB Reg 59(5)(b) HB Regs
33 **IS** Reg 62(3B) IS Regs
ESA Reg 132(6) ESA Regs
HB Reg 59(7) HB Regs
34 **IS** Regs 61, definition of 'period of study', and 62(3)(a) IS Regs
ESA Regs 131(1), definition of 'period of study', and 132(4)(a) ESA Regs
HB Regs 53, definition of 'period of study', and 59(5)(a) HB Regs
35 **IS** Reg 29(2B) IS Regs
JSA Reg 94(2B) JSA Regs
ESA Reg 91(4) ESA Regs
36 *Leeves v Chief Adjudication Officer*, reported as R(IS) 5/99; reg 31(1) HB Regs

4. Discretionary funds and other payments
37 **IS** Reg 61 IS Regs
ESA Reg 131 ESA Regs
HB Reg 53 HB Regs
All Definition of 'access funds'
38 **IS** Reg 68 IS Regs
ESA Reg 142 ESA Regs
HB Reg 68 HB Regs
39 **IS** Reg 68(4) IS Regs
ESA Reg 2 ESA Regs
40 **IS** Reg 66B IS Regs
ESA Reg 138 ESA Regs
HB Reg 65 HB Regs
41 **IS** Reg 41(6) IS Regs
ESA Reg 105(4) ESA Regs
HB Reg 41(4) HB Regs
42 **IS** Sch 9 para 13(2) IS Regs
ESA Sch 8 para 15(2) ESA Regs
HB Sch 5 para 13(2) HB Regs
43 **IS** Sch 9 para 13(1)(c) IS Regs
ESA Sch 8 para 15(1)(c) ESA Regs
HB Sch 5 para 13(1)(c) HB Regs

Chapter 17: How income affects means-tested benefits
Notes

44 **IS** Regs 51(3)(a)(ii) or 62(2)(a) IS Regs
JSA Regs 113(3)(a)(ii) or 131(2)(a) JSA Regs
ESA Regs 107(3)(c) or 132(2)(a) ESA Regs
HB Regs 49(3)(b) or 59(2)(a) HB Regs

6. Benefits and tax credits
45 The Social Security (Scotland) Act 2018 (Consequential Modifications) Order 2018, No.872

Chapter 18

How income affects tax credits

This chapter covers:
1. Working out your income (below)
2. Grants and loans (p162)
3. Earnings (p163)
4. Benefits (p163)
5. Other income (p164)

This chapter explains how HM Revenue and Customs treats your income when working out your entitlement to tax credits. For how income affects universal credit, see Chapter 16, and for how income affects income support, income-based jobseeker's allowance, income-related employment and support allowance and housing benefit, see Chapter 17.

Basic facts
– Most student income is ignored when working out your entitlement to tax credits.
– Some benefits and other income are taken into account.
– Gross earnings are counted as income.

1. Working out your income

While you are on income support (IS), income-based jobseeker's allowance, income-related employment and support allowance or pension credit, you are entitled to maximum tax credits without any income test. If you are not on these benefits, the tax credit assessment is based on income over a full tax year, 6 April to 5 April. When you claim, HM Revenue and Customs (HMRC) uses your income from the previous complete tax year. If you are claiming between 6 April 2019 and 5 April 2020, it uses income from 6 April 2018 to 5 April 2019. **Note:** although your income from a previous year is used in the initial assessment, all other relevant circumstances, such as the age of your child, are taken from the current year of the tax credit award.

Chapter 18: How income affects tax credits
1. Working out your income

Your tax credits are first assessed using the previous year's income, even if HMRC knows at the outset that your circumstances have changed. If you expect your income over the current tax year to be more than £2,500 lower or higher, tell HMRC and it reassesses your entitlement. If you do not tell HMRC, you will have an overpayment to pay back at the end of the tax year, or an underpayment of tax credits that you will get back as a lump sum. At the end of the tax year, HMRC sends you an annual review form to check whether your income and circumstances have stayed the same over the year. It reassesses your award for the previous year based on the current year's income plus £2,500 if it is more than £2,500 lower than in the previous year or, based on the current year's income less a disregard of £2,500, if it is more than £2,500 higher.

If your income increases by £2,500 or less since the previous tax year used to assess your claim, you do not need to tell HMRC as this does not affect the amount to which you are entitled. However, you should let HMRC know if the change means you are now eligible for working tax credit (WTC) or more WTC. Any increase is taken into account from the following April (April 2020 for an increase in the 2019/20 tax year), so it is important to tell HMRC of any increase by this date, otherwise you are likely to incur an overpayment.

If you have a partner, your claim is made jointly and her/his income counts as well as yours.

Unless you or your partner are working and eligible for WTC, your maximum child tax credit (CTC) is reduced if your income is above the threshold of £16,105 a year. If you are eligible for WTC, this threshold is £6,420. When working out your income, some income is disregarded.

Examples
Antonio is a mature student. He has one child, Eva. In the tax year April 2018 to April 2019 he was working full time earning £21,000. He started university in September 2018 and now his only income, apart from child benefit, is his student grants and loan. He gets the family element of CTC only, based on his earnings in the tax year 2018/19. Antonio phones the Tax Credit Helpline and gives details of his student support. HMRC reassesses his CTC based on this year's income plus £2,500 and awards him maximum CTC (one family element and one child element).

Kirsty was getting IS before she became a student. She now gets a student loan of £6,750, an independent students' bursary of £1,000, a lone parents' grant of £1,305, a childcare grant of £1,215, child support maintenance of £520 and child benefit. Her CTC is reassessed and she is awarded maximum CTC based on the IS she was getting in the tax year 2018/19. Although her income in 2019/20 has increased since 2018/19, only the lone parents' grant counts for tax credit purposes. Kirsty is still entitled to maximum CTC.

Chapter 18: How income affects tax credits
2. Grants and loans

2. Grants and loans

Most student grants and loans are ignored in the tax credit assessment except for the following, which are taken into account:[1]
- dependants' grant for adults;
- dependants' grant for children;
- lone parents' grant.[2]

The following grants and loans are disregarded.
   Higher education:
- tuition fees;
- postgraduate tuition fee loan;
- student loan;
- lone parents' childcare grant;
- care experienced students' bursary;
- care experienced accommodation grant;
- disabled students' allowance;
- travel expenses;
- young students' bursary;
- independent students' bursary;
- childcare fund;
- discretionary funds;
- nursing and midwifery student bursary.

Further education (FE):
- bursary maintenance allowance;
- care experienced students' bursary;
- education maintenance allowance;
- additional support needs for learning allowance;
- study expenses allowance;
- travel expenses allowance;
- lone parents' childcare grant;
- FE discretionary fund;
- childcare fund.

Any scholarship, exhibition, bursary or any other similar educational endowment is ignored if you are receiving full-time instruction (further or higher education) at an educational institution.[3]

A professional and career development loan is disregarded, except for any amount applied for or paid in respect of living expenses for the period supported by the loan.[4]

Example
Lauren is an undergraduate. She has one child aged 13. Her income for 2019/20 is:
– student loan;
– lone parents' grant;
– independent students' bursary;
– child benefit.
The student loan, independent students' bursary and child benefit are ignored for child tax credit (CTC). The lone parents' grant counts as income. Because this is less than the threshold of £16,105, Lauren is entitled to maximum CTC.

3. Earnings

Your gross earnings plus those of your partner are taken into account in the tax credit assessment. 'Gross earnings' means all income before any income tax or national insurance contributions are deducted. It also includes tips, overtime pay, taxable expenses and, ignoring the first £30,000, taxable payments related to the termination of employment such as redundancy pay.[5] If you make any contributions to a personal or occupational pension approved by HM Revenue and Customs, these should be disregarded.[6] The first £100 a week of statutory maternity, adoption, paternity and shared parental pay is disregarded, but payments above this are included.[7] Statutory sick pay is included in full.[8] Any payments that are exempt from income tax should generally be ignored for tax credit purposes.

For full details of the way earnings are treated, see CPAG's *Welfare Benefits and Tax Credits Handbook*.

4. Benefits

Generally, benefits that are not taxable are disregarded when calculating tax credits, and benefits that are taxable are included. For full details of the way social security benefits are treated, see CPAG's *Welfare Benefits and Tax Credits Handbook*.

Benefits taken into account in full include:
- carer's allowance (CA);
- contribution-based jobseeker's allowance (JSA);
- contributory employment and support allowance (ESA);
- long-term incapacity benefit (except pre-1995 awards);
- increases for a child or adult dependant paid with any of the above benefits.

Benefits completely disregarded include:[9]
- bereavement support payment;
- Best Start grant;
- CA supplement and young carer grant;[10]
- child benefit;
- disability living allowance;
- personal independence payment;
- income-related ESA;
- guardian's allowance;
- housing benefit;
- income support (except to strikers);
- income-based JSA;
- industrial injuries benefit;
- maternity allowance;
- funeral support payments;
- most war pensions;[11]
- increases for a child or adult dependant paid with any of the above benefits.

Benefits partly disregarded include state retirement pension (and private and occupational pensions) and widowed parent's allowance. These are included in tax credit calculations, although the first £300 of the total income from pensions, income from capital, and foreign income is disregarded.

5. Other income

What follows is a brief outline of how other income is treated. For further details, see CPAG's *Welfare Benefits and Tax Credits Handbook*.

Income from self-employment

Your taxable profits are taken into account less any personal pension contributions.

Savings and investments

There is no capital limit for tax credits. You are eligible whatever amount of savings you have and whatever the value of other capital. However, income generated from your savings or other capital is taken into account. For example, interest from bank accounts is taken into account, unless it is in a tax-free savings account. However, if you have no income from property or pensions, or foreign income, interest on savings or other capital is only taken into account if it is over £300 a year.

Property

Taxable rental income from property you let to tenants is taken into account, although you can rent a furnished room in your own home for up to £7,500 a year and this rental income is ignored. As with savings and investments, the capital value of any property is ignored, but any taxable rental income is included, although the first £300 of the total income from pensions, income from capital and foreign income is disregarded.[12]

Maintenance

Regular maintenance from an ex-partner is ignored, regardless of how the arrangement was made. Similarly, any support received from an ex-partner for your child(ren) is also ignored.[13]

Notes

2. **Grants and loans**
    1. Reg 8 TC(DCI) Regs
    2. Reg 8 TC(DCI) Regs refers only to a 'dependants' grant'. However, HMRC's intention seems to be to count the lone parents' grant also.
    3. Reg 9 TC(DCI) Regs
    4. Reg 19(c) Table 8 para 2 TC(DCI) Regs

3. **Earnings**
    5. Reg 4 TC(DCI) Regs
    6. Reg 3(7)(c) TC(DCI) Regs
    7. Reg 4(1)(h) TC(DCI) Regs
    8. Reg 4(1)(g) TC(DCI) Regs

4. **Benefits**
    9. Reg 7(3) TC(DCI) Regs
    10. The Tax Credits and Childcare (Miscellaneous Amendments) Regulations 2018, No.365
    11. Reg 5 TC(DCI) Regs

5. **Other income**
    12. Reg 11 TC(DCI) Regs
    13. Reg 19 Table 6 para 10 TC(DCI) Regs

19

Chapter 19

How income affects health benefits

This chapter covers:
1. Working out your income (below)
2. Grants and loans (p167)
3. Discretionary funds and other payments (p169)
4. Earnings (p170)
5. Benefits and tax credits (p170)
6. Maintenance (p171)
7. Savings and other capital (p171)

This chapter explains how your income is treated when working out your entitlement to health benefits under the NHS low income scheme (see p33).

If you are not exempt from healthcare costs (see Chapter 5) and have less than £16,000 a year in property, savings or other assessed income or capital, you are eligible to apply for at least some assistance.

Basic facts
– The NHS low income scheme helps with health costs if your income is low enough.
– Student loans and most grants count as income.
– Other income, such as earnings, some benefits and tax credits, is taken into account in the assessment.

1. Working out your income

The way that student income is taken into account for health benefits is broadly the same as for means-tested benefits.[1]

| Step one | Add together the annual income from your grants and loan. Include the maximum for which you are eligible. |
| Step two | Apply annual disregard. Deduct the disregarded amount of £693 for books, equipment and travel. |

Step three   Divide income throughout the year.
            Divide the annual amount of loan and grant income by 52 weeks, unless you are in the final or only year of your course, in which case you should divide by the number of weeks (Sunday to Saturday) from 1 August to the last day of your course.
Step four   **Weekly disregard.**
            Unlike the means-tested benefits assessment, there is no weekly disregard of £10 on the student loan, unless you receive a premium in your applicable amount, a disabled students' allowance because of deafness, or you are not a student but your partner is. If you fall into any of these categories, disregard £10.
Step five   **Add other income to weekly loan and grant amount. This total is the amount of income used in the health benefit calculation.**
            Add together any other weekly income (eg, from discretionary funds or a professional and career development loan), earnings (see p170), tariff income from capital (see p171), and benefits and tax credits (see p170). Ignore any amount that is disregarded.

2. Grants and loans

Grants

In general, grants intended for living costs are taken into account and grants for other costs are disregarded. For details of how discretionary funds are treated, see p169.

If you are *not* eligible for a student loan, the disregards for books, travel and equipment are deducted from your grant (see p166).

The following further education (FE) grants are disregarded:
- education maintenance allowance;
- additional support needs for learning allowance for disability costs;
- study expenses allowance if paid for books and equipment;
- travel expenses allowance;
- lone parents' childcare grant.

The following FE grants are taken into account:
- bursary maintenance allowance;
- care experienced students' bursary;
- dependants' allowance.

The following higher education (HE) grants are disregarded:
- young students' bursary;
- independent students' bursary;

Chapter 19: How income affects health benefits
2. Grants and loans

- lone parents' childcare grant;
- disabled students' allowance;
- travel expenses;
- tuition fees;
- childcare allowance.

The following HE grants are taken into account:
- care experienced students' bursary;
- care experienced accommodation grant;
- dependants' grant;
- lone parents' grant;
- nursing and midwifery bursary, single parents' allowance and dependants' allowance.

If you are a postgraduate student, take into account any research council or other maintenance grant and dependants' allowances. Grants for living costs are treated in the same way as those for undergraduates.

Example
Ramla is on a one-year FE course and gets a bursary of £4,247.97 for a 43-week course. Her income is her bursary minus the £693 disregard, divided by 43. This is £82.67 a week.

Student loan

Student loan income includes the maximum loan available, not including any hardship loan.[2] This is taken into account as your income whether or not you apply for it.

Examples
Madhu is 20 and is a second-year undergraduate. She gets a student loan of £5,750 and a young students' bursary of £2,000. The bursary is disregarded. Six hundred and ninety-three pounds is disregarded from the student loan and the result is divided by 52 weeks. Her total weekly income is £97.25.

Lewis is 26 and is a second-year undergraduate. He gets a student loan of £6,750 and an independent students' bursary of £1,000. He also works part time, earning £55 a week. The bursary is disregarded. Six hundred and ninety-three pounds is disregarded from the student loan and the result is divided by 52 weeks, giving a weekly income from his student loan of £116.48. Five pounds of his earnings is disregarded (see p170) and £50 a week is taken into account. His total weekly income is £166.48.

3. Discretionary funds and other payments

Discretionary funds

Discretionary support provided when you are in financial difficulty is treated differently from other student grants and loans. This support includes:
- higher education (HE) discretionary fund;
- further education (FE) discretionary fund.

In general, if the payment is for certain living costs, it is taken into account in full if it counts as capital, or with up to a £20 a week disregard if it counts as income. If the payment is for other costs, it is disregarded. Ask your college/university for a letter saying what the payment is for and how it is paid.

Lump-sum payments count as capital. Regular payments count as income.

The FE and HE childcare funds are disregarded.

Lump-sum payments

Lump-sum payments are taken into account as capital if they are intended and used for food, ordinary clothing or footwear, household fuel, rent met by housing benefit (HB), housing costs met by income support (IS), income-based jobseeker's allowance (JSA) or income-related employment and support allowance (ESA), council tax or water charges. Payments for anything else are disregarded. Although taken into account as capital, this only affects your entitlement if it brings your capital above the lower limit. See p171 for details.

Regular payments

Regular payments are taken into account as income if they are intended and used for food, ordinary clothing or footwear, household fuel, rent met by HB, housing costs met by IS, income-based JSA or income-related ESA, council tax or water charges. Up to £20 a week is disregarded. You cannot get the £20 disregard in full as well as the full disregards available on a student loan or voluntary and charitable payments (or on widowed parent's allowance or war pensions). If you get one of these other payments as well as a discretionary fund payment, your maximum weekly disregard is £20.

For example, if you have a student loan (and are eligible for the £10 disregard) and regular payments from the HE discretionary fund, £10 a week is disregarded from each. If you also receive regular payments from a charity, these count in full because you have already used up your £20 disregard on the loan and the discretionary fund payment.

Regular payments intended and used for anything else, such as childcare expenses, are completely disregarded.

Chapter 19: How income affects health benefits
5. Benefits and tax credits

Other payments

Voluntary or charitable payments

Regular voluntary or charitable payments are treated as income, with a disregard of up to £20 a week.[3] One-off or lump-sum voluntary or charitable payments are treated as capital.

Professional and career development loans

Professional and career development loans are always treated as income, not capital, irrespective of how they are paid. The loan is taken into account if it is intended and used for food, ordinary clothing or footwear, household fuel, rent met by HB, housing costs met by IS, income-based JSA or income-related ESA, council tax or water charges. Once the period of education supported by the loan is completed, the loan is disregarded altogether, whatever it was originally intended for.

4. Earnings

Your earnings and the earnings of your partner are taken into account in the health benefits assessment. Your net weekly earnings are taken into account – ie, after deducting:
- income tax;
- class 1 national insurance contributions;
- half of any contribution you make towards a personal or occupational pension.

There is also an earnings disregard of £5, £10 or £20 per week, as for income support (see p155), with a modification that allows a £20 disregard if you get a disability premium or if you or your partner are over 60. The earnings disregard is increased to the whole of the earnings if you are on contributory employment and support allowance and doing permitted work.[4]

5. Benefits and tax credits

If you receive income support (IS), income-based jobseeker's allowance (JSA), income-related employment and support allowance (ESA) or child tax credit (CTC) and have a household income of no more than £15,276, you automatically get free health benefits (see Chapter 5). You may also qualify if you get universal credit (see p32).

Housing benefit is effectively disregarded, as the NHS Business Services Authority only takes into account the rent paid by you directly when determining need.

Benefits and tax credits taken into account in full include:
- carer's allowance (CA);
- contribution-based JSA;
- contributory ESA;
- incapacity benefit;
- most industrial injuries benefits;
- retirement pension;
- working tax credit.

Benefits and tax credits completely disregarded include:
- attendance allowance;
- Best Start grant;
- CA supplement and young carer grant;[5]
- child benefit;
- CTC;
- disability living allowance;
- personal independence payment;
- funeral support payments.

Benefits and tax credits partly disregarded include widowed parent's allowance, which has £10 a week disregarded. **Note:** you do not receive this disregard if you already have £10 disregarded from a student loan or £20 disregarded from discretionary fund payments.

6. Maintenance

Regular child maintenance payments are disregarded and lump sums are treated as capital.

7. Savings and other capital

There are limits on the amount of savings and other capital you can have and still claim health benefits.

You cannot get health benefits if your savings and other capital are above £16,000.

If your capital is £6,000 or less, it does not affect your claim at all. If your capital is between £6,000.01 and £16,000, you are treated as though you have an income from this capital of £1 a week for every £250 (or part of £250) between these amounts. This is referred to as 'tariff income'. For example, if you have savings of £6,525, your tariff income is £3 a week.

Chapter 19: How income affects health benefits
Notes

Notes

1. **Working out your income**
   1 NHS(TERC)(S) Regs, as amended (most recently in 2015 by SI No.333)

2. **Grants and loans**
   2 The National Health Service (Travelling Expenses and Remission of Charges) (Scotland) (No.2) Amendment Regulations 2013, No.327

3. **Discretionary funds and other payments**
   3 The National Health Service (Travelling Expenses and Remission of Charges) (Scotland) Amendment (No.3) Regulations 2007, No.391

4. **Earnings**
   4 The National Health Service (Travelling Expenses and Remission of Charges) (Scotland) Amendment (No.3) Regulations 2008, No.390

5. **Benefits and tax credits**
   5 The Social Security (Scotland) Act 2018 (Consequential Modifications) Order 2018, No.872

Part 4
Other matters

Chapter 20

Council tax

This chapter covers:
1. What is council tax (below)
2. Who pays council tax (p176)
3. Council tax reduction (p180)
4. Second adult rebate (p181)

Basic facts

– Council tax is a local tax on residential dwellings.
– You do not pay council tax if you are under 18.
– Students sharing accommodation solely with other students do not pay council tax.
– Students sharing accommodation with non-students usually do not pay council tax.
– Students who own the home in which they live are liable, but may be exempt or get a discount or second adult rebate.
– Part-time students can apply for a council tax reduction. A full-time student liable to pay council tax can apply for a council tax reduction in some circumstances.

1. What is council tax

Council tax is a tax on residential dwellings paid to the local authority. It includes an amount for water and sewerage. There is one amount to pay and one bill for each dwelling unless it is exempt from council tax. A 'dwelling' includes a self-contained flat.

Each dwelling is allocated a valuation band from A to H based on property values in 1991. Council tax is lowest for those in Band A.

Some dwellings are exempt from council tax. If the dwelling is exempt, there is no council tax to pay for anyone who lives there or for a non-resident owner. There are exemptions specifically for students.

Although non-student flat/house sharers are normally jointly liable for the bill, full-time students are not usually liable to pay council tax unless they own the property. Those liable for council tax may get a discount or exemption if they live alone or if they share with students. The amount to pay may be further reduced if the person is eligible for council tax reduction or second adult rebate (see pp180–81).

2. Who pays council tax

If you are a student, there are two main ways in which you are exempt from paying council tax.
- The accommodation you live in may be exempt (see p178).
- You may not be liable to pay any council tax (see p179).

If neither of these applies, you may be able to reduce your council tax bill.
- You may be able to get a discount (see p180).
- You may be able to get council tax reduction or second adult rebate (see pp180–81).

Who counts as a student

If you are aged under 20, whether you count as a student for council tax purposes depends on whether you are on a further or higher education course. For older students, one rule applies whatever level of course you do. If you are an 'articulating' student of any age, you may count as a student between courses (see p178).

Under 20 in further education

You are regarded as a 'student' for council tax purposes if you are aged under 20 and on a further education (FE) course of more than 12 hours a week, which lasts more than three months.[1]

An FE course is one below the level of a degree, Higher National Certificate (HNC), Higher National Diploma (HND) or Scottish Vocational Qualification (SVQ) level 4. It includes National Qualifications to Advanced Higher level, A levels and National Certificates. It does not include:
- further training of teachers or youth or community workers;[2]
- evening classes;[3]
- correspondence courses;[4]
- courses attended if you are a trainee on a youth training course or an apprentice.[5]

The hours that count are those required by the course rather than those you actually do, if they are different.

To work out your hours, average out over term times the hours required under the course for tuition, supervised study, exams, and supervised exercise, experiment, project and practical work.[6] You can add together hours spent on more than one course if these are all at the same college.[7]

You are regarded as a student for each day from the day you start the course until the day you complete it, abandon it or are dismissed from it.[8] So you count as a student during term times, during short vacations at Christmas and Easter and during the summer if your course continues after the summer. If your course ends in the summer and you begin a different one in the autumn, you do not count as a student in the summer between courses.[9] However, you might be able to get a discount (see p180).

> **Example**
> Drew is 18 and taking three Highers at college. Including his classes, exams and supervised study, his course hours are 18 a week. He is a student for council tax purposes.

Under 20 in higher education
The rules are the same as those for people aged 20 or over (see below).

20 or over in further or higher education
If you are aged 20 or over, you are regarded as a 'student' for council tax purposes if the course requires you to undertake periods of study, tuition or work experience of at least 24 weeks each academic year, for an average of at least 21 hours a week.[10] This includes distance learning.

To count as a student, you must be enrolled on a course with an educational institution. You are a student from the day you begin the course until the day you complete it, abandon it or are no longer permitted by the educational institution to attend.[11] So if you take time out and are not enrolled on the course during this period, you do not count as a student for council tax purposes and may become liable for council tax. If this is the case, check whether you can get council tax reduction (see p180). On the other hand, if you take time out but are still enrolled on the course, you continue to count as a student, provided you have not abandoned it completely and the institution has not said you can no longer attend the course. Because the law says you are not a student if you are 'no longer permitted by the institution to attend', this suggests that your dismissal from the course must be final. So you could argue that if you are temporarily suspended from the course but still registered, you still count as a student.

Your college or university determines the number of hours. You may need evidence from it to prove to the local authority that you count as a student. Colleges and universities are required to provide you with a certificate if you ask for one while you are a student or up to a year after you leave the course.[12] After that, they may still give you a certificate, but they are not legally required to do so. The certificate must contain:[13]
- the name and address of the institution;
- your full name;
- your term-time address and home address (if known by the institution);

- a statement that you are (or were) a student – ie, that you are enrolled on a course requiring attendance of at least 24 weeks a year and study of at least 21 hours a week; *and*
- the date you became a student and the date your course ends.

Articulating or direct entry students

You count as a student if you have finished an HNC or HND course and have an offer of a place directly into the second or third year of a degree course.[14] To qualify, if you have completed a full-time HNC course in the last six months, you must have an offer of a place in the second year of a full-time degree course starting within this period. The same applies if you have completed a full-time HND course in the last six months, except that the offer must be of a place in the third year of a full-time degree course. See p177 for the definition of 'full-time course'.

If you meet these rules but do not start the degree course, you do not count as a student for the period between the courses.

Exempt dwellings

A dwelling is exempt from council tax if all the people who occupy it are in any of the following categories:[15]
- a student, or her/his overseas partner if s/he entered the UK on a visa that prohibits her/him from working or claiming benefits. If the partner has the right to work but not to claim benefits, arguably s/he should come under this exemption; *or*
- a care leaver aged 18–25; *or*
- someone under age 18; *or*
- someone under age 20 who left further education at school or college after 30 April – this only applies between 1 May and 31 October of the year s/he left school or college; *or*
- someone who is 'severely mentally impaired'.

Halls of residence are also exempt dwellings. This applies if the hall of residence is mainly for students and is owned and managed by an educational institution, or where there is an agreement that the educational institution can nominate the majority of those who can stay in the accommodation.[16]

An unoccupied dwelling is exempt for up to four months if it is the main residence of a student (and not of anyone else who is not a student) and it was last occupied by one or more students. This allows an exemption to continue – eg, through the summer vacation. If you are liable for council tax (and anyone who is jointly liable with you is also a student) and the dwelling is no one's main residence, the dwelling is exempt without a time limit.

If the dwelling is exempt, there is no council tax or council water charge to pay.[17]

There are a number of other exemptions that are not specifically aimed at students. For details, see CPAG's *Council Tax Handbook*.

Who is liable for council tax

Very few students are liable to pay council tax. Normally, either the dwelling is exempt because everyone who lives there is a student, or the non-students in the household are solely liable for the council tax.

If the dwelling is not exempt from council tax, at least one person is liable for the bill. There is a hierarchy to determine liability – the first person in the hierarchy is the one who is liable to pay. If there are two or more people at the same level, they are usually jointly liable, but there is an exception for students.

Council tax liability hierarchy
Resident owner
Resident tenant
Resident statutory, statutory assured or secure tenant
Resident sub-tenant
Other resident
Non-resident owner unless there is a non-resident tenant or a non-resident sub-tenant, either of whom have a lease of six months or more

If students share accommodation with non-students who are at the same level in the hierarchy, the non-students are liable but the students are not.[18]

Examples
Three students, Rahul, Will and Jameel, share a flat as joint tenants. While they are all students, the flat is exempt and there is no council tax to pay. Will drops out of his course. The flat is no longer exempt. Will is solely liable for the whole council tax bill (although there is a discount). Rahul and Jameel are not liable for any council tax. Will should apply for a council tax reduction if his income is low.

Christine is studying full time and owns the flat she lives in. She rents a room to a friend who is not a student. Christine is liable for the council tax. She gets a 25 per cent discount on the bill. Her friend is not liable for any council tax.

Raj is studying full time and owns the flat he lives in. He rents a room to a friend who is also a student. Raj is liable for the council tax, but as both of them are students, the flat is exempt and the bill is, therefore, nil.

Couples

Normally, couples who live together are jointly liable for the council tax. Students, however, are exempt from this rule. If you are a student and have a non-student partner who is liable for council tax, you are not jointly liable with her/him.[19]

Discounts

The full council tax bill assumes that there are two adults living in the dwelling. You get a discount of 25 per cent if there is only one person living there. Some people are disregarded when counting how many live in the dwelling. They are described as 'invisible' or as having a 'status discount'. If someone is disregarded in this way and there is no one, or only one adult counted as, living in the property, you get a discount of 50 per cent or 25 per cent. The discount is on the water charge, as well as the council tax charge.[20]

The following people are disregarded in this way:[21]
- anyone under 18 years old;
- anyone aged 18 or 19 for whom child benefit is payable;
- students;
- a student's partner from overseas if s/he entered the UK on a visa that prohibits her/him from working or claiming benefits;
- someone under age 20 who was on a non-advanced course of education and who left school or college after 1 May – the status discount lasts from 1 May until 31 October;
- student nurses – ie, those studying for registration;
- apprentices training for an SVQ and on low pay;
- a care leaver aged 18–25, who was looked after on or after her/his 16th birthday and is no longer looked after;
- others – eg, carers, hospital patients and trainees. See CPAG's *Council Tax Handbook* for details.

Disability reduction

The council tax bill is reduced to the valuation band below your own band if you, or anyone else (adult or child) who is resident in the dwelling, are substantially and permanently disabled and you use a wheelchair indoors or need an extra room.

3. Council tax reduction

Council tax reduction is administered by local authorities and helps you pay the council tax. To get council tax reduction, you must meet all the following conditions.[22]

- You are liable for council tax. Most students are not liable for council tax and have no need to apply for a reduction.
- You do not count as a student, or you count as a student but are still eligible for council tax reduction (see below).
- You are 'habitually resident' in the UK, Ireland, Channel Islands or the Isle of Man, have a 'right to reside' in the UK, and are not a 'person subject to immigration control'. These terms are explained in CPAG's *Welfare Benefits and Tax Credits Handbook*.
- You have no more than £16,000 capital. There is no capital limit if you are getting pension credit (PC) guarantee credit (see p157).
- Your income is low enough. Council tax reduction is means tested, so the amount you get depends on how much income you have.

Students eligible for council tax reduction

Part-time students are eligible for council tax reduction. If you are a full-time student, you are not eligible unless:[23]
- you are a qualifying young person for child benefit purposes (see p9); *or*
- you are under 22 on a course of further education which you started when you were under 21; *or*
- you are a full-time student in higher education, or aged 19 or over in further education and:
  - you get universal credit, income support, income-based jobseeker's allowance or income-related employment and support allowance; *or*
  - you have a child; *or*
  - you are a disabled student; *or*
  - you have reached pension age.

The way 'full-time student' is defined is the same as for housing benefit (HB – see p38).[24] **Note:** it is not the same as the definition for council tax described in this chapter.

You can get an application form for council tax reduction from the local authority.

4. Second adult rebate

All students who are liable for council tax can claim second adult rebate. The law refers to this as 'alternative maximum council tax reduction'. It is intended for people whose bill is higher because they live with others who cannot get a status discount but who cannot make a full contribution towards a share of the bill. You can only get a second adult rebate if you live with others who are not students. If all of you are students, you cannot get this rebate.

Chapter 20: Council tax
4. Second adult rebate

Whether or not you get a rebate depends on the income of the people who share with you. Your own income or capital is ignored.

You can get a second adult rebate if:[25]
- you are liable for council tax; *and*
- you have a 'second adult' (see below) living with you; *and*
- the second adult is on universal credit (UC), income support (IS), income-based jobseeker's allowance (JSA), income-related employment and support allowance (ESA) or pension credit (PC), or has a low income; *and*
- you do not get rent from a tenant or sub-tenant (arguably, rent from students or others who have a status discount should not disbar you from getting second adult rebate);[26] *and*
- if you are in a couple, one or both of you are students or have a status discount for some other reason; *and*
- if you are jointly liable for the council tax, all of those jointly liable are (or all but one are) students or have a status discount for some other reason.

Second adult
A **'second adult'** is someone aged 18 or over who is a non-dependant – ie, someone who lives with you on a non-commercial basis, is not a student, and does not have a status discount for any other reason.

If you are eligible for second adult rebate and for council tax reduction, the local authority decides which is worth the most to you. You cannot get both at the same time. If you get a second adult rebate, you get a reduction of 100 per cent if the second adult(s) gets IS, income-based JSA, income-related ESA, PC or UC and everyone else is a full-time student,[27] or 25 per cent, 15 per cent or 7.5 per cent depending on the income of the second adult(s).

Examples
Terry lives with his daughter, Minnie, aged 22. Terry is a full-time student. Minnie is claiming JSA. Terry rents the house from a housing association. Terry can claim second adult rebate of 100 per cent. Minnie is the second adult.

Dean is a student and he owns the flat he shares with his brother, Steve. Steve is aged 19 and works for the minimum wage. Dean can claim second adult rebate. Steve is the second adult.

Chapter 20: Council tax Notes

Notes

2. Who pays council tax
1 Art 6(1)(b) and Sch 1 para 1(a) CT(D)(S)CAO
2 Sch 1 para 2 CT(D)(S)CAO
3 Sch 1 para 1(d) CT(D)(S)CAO
4 Sch 1 para 1(c) CT(D)(S)CAO
5 Art 6(3)(c) CT(D)(S)CAO
6 Art 2, definitions of 'relevant number of hours' and 'relevant activities', CT(D)(S)CAO
7 Art 6(3)(a) CT(D)(S)CAO
8 Art 2, definition of 'the relevant period', CT(D)(S)CAO
9 Art 6(3)(b) CT(D)(S)CAO
10 Art 6(4)(c) CT(D)(S)CAO
11 Arts 2, definition of 'the relevant period', and 6(4)(e) CT(D)(S)CAO
12 Sch 1 para 5 LGFA 1992
13 Art 9 CT(D)(S)CAO
14 Art 6(1)(d) and (e) CT(D)(S)CAO
15 Sch 1 para 10 The Council Tax (Exempt Dwellings) (Scotland) Order 1997, No.728
16 Sch 1 para 16 The Council Tax (Exempt Dwellings) (Scotland) Order 1997, No.728
17 Sch 11 para 7(11) LGFA 1992
18 s75(4) LGFA 1992, as amended by s4 Education (Graduate Endowment and Student Support) (Scotland) Act 2001
19 s77 LGFA 1992, as amended by s4 Education (Graduate Endowment and Student Support) (Scotland) Act 2001
20 Sch 11 para 11 LGFA 1992
21 CT(D)(S)CAO; The Council Tax (Discounts) (Scotland) Regulations 1992, No.1409

3. Council tax reduction
22 Regs 14, 16, 19 and 42 CTR(S) Regs
23 Reg 20 CTR(S) Regs
24 Reg 2 CTR(S) Regs

4. Second adult rebate
25 Reg 78 and Sch 2 CTR(S) Regs
26 s131(6)(a) and (7) SSCBA 1992
27 Sch 5 para CTR(S) Regs

Chapter 21

Time out from studies

This chapter covers:
1. Ill health (below)
2. Pregnancy and children (p187)
3. Carers (p188)
4. Re-sits (p188)
5. Time out for other reasons (p188)

Basic facts
- Students may be able to receive student support or get social security benefits during periods of absence from their course.
- Support is usually only available if you have taken time out because you are ill or pregnant, or because you have to care for someone.
- Support may also be available once you have recovered from your illness or your caring responsibilities have ceased and you are waiting to return to your course.

1. Ill health

Full-time students

Which benefits you are eligible for depends on how long you have been ill, your age, whether you have paid any national insurance (NI) contributions, and whether you need personal care or have mobility difficulties. Once you have recovered, you may be able to get universal credit (UC) or, occasionally, jobseeker's allowance (JSA) until you can return to your course.

You usually still count as a full-time student when taking time out of your course, unless you have completely abandoned or been dismissed from it (but see p188 for when this may not apply).[1]

Note: if you have to take time out from your studies because you are ill, you cannot usually make a new claim for income-related employment and support allowance (ESA) or housing benefit (HB), as these benefits are in the process of being replaced by UC. However, an exception applies if you get, or got in the past month (and continue to satisfy the rules for it), a severe disability premium (see

Chapter 21: Time out from studies
1. Ill health

p20) in your ESA, income support, income-based JSA or HB, or (for HB only) you are in certain specified or temporary accommodation (see p37).

From the start of your ill health
If you have paid sufficient NI contributions in recent years, you are eligible for contributory ESA after seven 'waiting days' (see Chapter 4).

From three months
You can claim personal independence payment (PIP) if you need help getting around or with daily living activities because of a disability. You are eligible for this after three months if your disability is likely to last at least another nine months.

You can claim UC if you get PIP or disability living allowance (DLA) and have 'limited capability for work'. Your claim for UC may be refused outright if you do not already have limited capability for work. You can claim contributory ESA in order to establish that you have limited capability for work (although you do not have to get any ESA to qualify in this way). Once you are found to have limited capability for work for ESA (and you also get PIP or DLA), you are then eligible for UC.

If you get PIP or DLA, you may also be eligible for income-related ESA and for HB to help with your rent (if you can make a new claim for these benefits – see p20 and p37).

From 28 weeks
Once you have had 'limited capability for work' for 28 weeks, you can claim HB to help with your rent (if you can make a new claim for this – see p37).

The 28-week period runs from the day your limited capability for work begins, not from the day you leave your course. See p23 for how limited capability for work is assessed. You do not need to have been working to count as having limited capability for work. **Note:** you can have limited capability for work but still be able to study, so HB can continue when you return to college or university.

Example
Sean is ill and takes time out of his course. He is not eligible for PIP, and has not worked enough to qualify for contributory ESA. He gets no benefits until he has been ill for 28 weeks, when he can claim HB (because he lives in temporary accommodation). He makes a claim for ESA, supported by a backdated medical certificate, in order to establish his limited capability for work, and also fills in a claim form for HB.

Once you have recovered
Once you have recovered, you may need to wait some time to be readmitted to your course. During this time you can claim UC (or JSA and HB if you can make a new claim for these benefits – see p68 and p37).[2]

Chapter 21: Time out from studies
1. Ill health

You can claim for up to one year from the day you recover until the day the college or university agrees you can return to your course. You are not eligible if you get a grant or loan during this time. Once the student support stops, you can claim benefit.

Student support

Although payment of your student loan can be suspended after 60 days' absence because of ill health, the Student Awards Agency Scotland (SAAS) has the discretion to continue to pay you until the end of the academic year.

Your college or university should tell SAAS the reason you have suspended your studies.

If you need to repeat a year for health reasons, discretionary repeat-year funding may be available. Alternatively, you may get funding for one extra year for whatever reason, although this depends on your previous study.

If you select the repeat-year funding box on your application, SAAS contacts you to tell you if it needs additional information.

If you take time out from your course because of ill health and are not paid a student loan during this time, the unpaid student loan does not count as 'notional' income when calculating your ESA.[3] For UC and HB, the unpaid loan is arguably not counted as 'notional' income, because payment of it is discretionary.

Part-time students

If you are a part-time student, you can claim UC (or, sometimes, income-related ESA –see p20) as soon as you are ill or disabled, whether or not you get PIP or DLA.

From the start of your ill health

If you are already getting UC, you can submit a fit note if you become ill or disabled. If you are already getting JSA, you can continue to do so for up to 13 weeks. After that, you must claim ESA instead.

You can claim contributory ESA if you have paid sufficient NI contributions. In some cases, you can claim income-related ESA (see p20) and HB (see p37).

From three months

You can claim PIP if you need help getting around or with daily living activities because of a disability. You are eligible for this after three months if your disability is likely to last at least another nine months.

Once you have recovered

You can claim UC (or, sometimes, JSA – see p68).

2. Pregnancy and children

There is no provision for pregnant full-time students to claim universal credit (UC), income support (IS) or housing benefit (HB).

If you are a part-time student, you can get UC and you will have no work-related requirements from 11 weeks before your expected week of childbirth.

If you have an employer, you may be able to get statutory maternity pay. If you are not working now but have worked recently, you may be able to get maternity allowance.

Once the baby is born, there are various benefits you can claim. You can also get a 'baby box' from the Scottish government, containing basic items for a newborn baby.[4]

Nursing and midwifery students can continue to receive their bursary for a period of up to 45 weeks' maternity leave.

Lone parents

Once the baby is born, if you are a lone parent studying full time you can claim:
- a Best Start grant, if you get UC or certain other benefits, or you are under 18 (see p114) (see www.cpag.org.uk/scottish-benefits/best-start-grant). Claims must be made within six months of the birth or, in some cases, before the birth;
- Best Start foods (see p115).

Fathers and partners

If your partner has had a baby and you have an employer, you may be able to claim statutory paternity pay. You can claim if you are the child's father or the mother's partner and you will be caring for the baby or the mother. You may also be able to claim statutory shared parental pay.

Couples

Throughout the course, including in the summer vacation, a full-time student couple (ie, both partners are students) with a child can claim:
- child benefit;
- UC;
- Best Start foods (see p115).

Couples can also claim a Best Start grant if one partner gets a qualifying benefit (see p114).

3. Carers

If you are a full-time student, you cannot claim universal credit (UC) or get income support (IS) while you are looking after someone who is ill or disabled. You cannot usually claim carer's allowance (CA), but you may be able to if you have had to interrupt your studies and the interruption is not temporary (see p4).

Part-time students can claim UC (or IS in some cases – see p51) and CA.

If you are a full-time student, you may have to stop your course while you are caring. If you have to wait to return to it once your caring responsibilities have ended, you can claim UC. You can claim for up to a year until the day from when your institution agrees you can return to your course. You are not eligible if you get a grant or loan during this time.

4. Re-sits

If you are a full-time student taking time out to re-sit exams, you are still treated as a student during your absence from the course. You cannot claim universal credit (UC), income support (IS), jobseeker's allowance (JSA), income-related employment and support allowance (ESA) or housing benefit during this time, unless you would be eligible anyway as a student – eg, as a lone parent. However, if you are taking professional qualifications set by a professional institute or some other body unconnected to your own college or university, you may be able to claim UC while taking time out for re-sits. You may need to appeal and argue that caselaw supports your getting benefit.[5]

If your university allows you to 'register with attendance', you may be able to get a student loan and grant for living costs from the Student Awards Agency Scotland (SAAS) during a re-sit year. 'Registering with attendance' means you are registered as a full-time student, but you attend your course on a part-time basis for a year. SAAS does not pay your tuition fees or give you a bursary. If you are eligible for benefit, you may be better off being in 'academic suspension' for the year: you cannot get a loan, but you can claim UC (if you are a student who can get UC).

Note: you also continue to count as a full-time student if you are doing re-sits after the official end date of your course.[6]

5. Time out for other reasons

If you take time out of your course for another reason, you usually still count as a full-time student, with no additional entitlement to benefits during your time out. However, if you are on a modular course and take a full year (or more) out of

Chapter 21: Time out from studies
Notes

the course, you may no longer count as a student and may therefore be able to claim universal credit under the normal (non-student) rules.[7]

Notes

1. **Ill health**
   1 **UC** Reg 13(1)(a) UC Regs
   ESA Reg 2(1), definition of 'period of study', ESA Regs
   HB Reg 53(2) HB Regs
   2 **UC** Reg 13(4) UC Regs
   JSA Reg 1(3D) JSA Regs; para 30209 DMG
   HB Reg 56(6) HB Regs
   3 Reg 137(4A) ESA Regs

2. **Pregnancy and children**
   4 https://news.gov.scot/news/registration-for-baby-box-will-begin-in-june

4. **Re-sits**
   5 R(JSA) 2/02
   6 **UC** Reg 13(2)(a) UC Regs
   IS Reg 61(3) IS Regs; para 30236 DMG

5. **Time out for other reasons**
   7 *RVS v SSWP* [2019] UKUT 102 (AAC)

Appendices

Appendices

Appendix 1
Information and advice

Publications

The following books are available from CPAG, 30 Micawber Street, London N1 7TB, Tel: 020 7812 5236. You can also order online, and find details of CPAG's other handbooks and online subscription services, and details of the prices for members and Citizens Advice at https://cpag.org.uk/shop.

Welfare Benefits and Tax Credits Handbook 2019/20 (April 2019): £61 (£51.85 members and Citizens Advice)/£15 claimants)

Benefit and Tax Credit Rates Poster 2019/20: £7

Universal Credit: what you need to know, 5th edition (February 2019): £15 (£12.75 members and Citizens Advice)

Council Tax Handbook, 12th edition (December 2018): £26 (£22.10 members and Citizens Advice)

Fuel Rights Handbook, 19th edition (March 2019): £29 (£24.65 members and Citizens Advice)

Children's Handbook Scotland, 12th edition (autumn 2019): £28 (£23.80 members and Citizens Advice)

Disability Rights Handbook 2019/20 (April 2019): £35 (published by Disability Rights UK)

Student Support and Benefits Handbook: England, Wales and Northern Ireland 2019/20 (autumn 2019): £28 (£23.80 members and Citizens Advice)

Appendix 1: Information and advice

Official guidance

The following guidance, used by decision makers in the DWP and local authorities, is available at www.gov.uk. It has no legal standing, so you cannot quote it in an appeal, but it can be useful to refer decision makers to it if you want a decision overturned by an internal revision or supersession.

Advice for Decision Making (for universal credit and other benefits introduced from April 2013)

Decision Makers' Guide

Housing Benefit and Council Tax Benefit Guidance Manual

Legislation

UK legislation
All the legislation listed in Appendix 3 can be found at www.legislation.gov.uk. Most is updated.

Social Security Legislation, Volumes 1 to 5
Published by Sweet and Maxwell, these volumes contain updated Acts and regulations covering social security and tax credits with explanatory commentary. They are available from CPAG.

CPAG's Housing Benefit and Council Tax Reduction Legislation
Published by CPAG, this contains updated Acts and regulations and a detailed commentary.

Decisions of the Upper Tribunal
Reported and unreported decisions are available from www.gov.uk/administrative-appeals-tribunal-decisions.

Advice

Contact your student services department, student association, bursaries office or the National Association of Student Money Advisers (www.nasma.org.uk) for advice on studying and claiming benefits.

Appendix 2
Useful addresses

CPAG in Scotland
Unit 9, Ladywell
94 Duke Street
Glasgow G4 0UW
Tel: 0141 552 3303
Advice line for advisers only: 0141 552 0552
(Mon–Thurs, 10am–4pm; Fri, 10am–12 noon)
advice@cpagscotland.org.uk
https://cpag.org.uk/scotland

CPAG in Scotland provides an advice, information and training service for advisers.

SDS Individual Training Accounts
www.myworldofwork.co.uk/learn-and-train/sds-individual-training-accounts-ita

Skills Development Scotland
www.myworldofwork.co.uk/learn-and-train/funding

Skills Development Scotland's 'my world of work' webpages contain funding information and can be used by both students and advisers.

Lead Scotland
Room B05, Edinburgh Napier University
Merchiston Campus
14 Colinton Road
Edinburgh EH10 5DT
Freephone helpline: 0800 999 2568 (Mon–Wed, 2–5pm; Thurs, 2.30–5.30pm)
info@lead.org.uk
www.lead.org.uk

Lead Scotland is a charity that enables disabled adults and carers to access learning opportunities.

Appendix 2: Useful addresses

National Union of Students Scotland
1 Papermill Wynd
McDonald Road
Edinburgh EH7 4QL
Tel: 0300 303 8602
mail@nus-scotland.org.uk
www.nus.org.uk

Scottish Funding Council
97 Haymarket Terrace
Edinburgh EH12 5HD
Tel: 0131 313 6500
enquiries@sfc.ac.uk
www.sfc.ac.uk

Scottish Social Services Council
Compass House
11 Riverside Drive
Dundee DD1 4NY
Tel: 0345 603 0891
enquiries@sssc.uk.com
www.sssc.uk.com

Student Awards Agency Scotland
Saughton House
Broomhouse Drive
Edinburgh EH11 3UT
Tel: 0300 555 0505
www.saas.gov.uk

Student Loans Company
100 Bothwell Street
Glasgow G2 7JD
Tel: 0300 100 0609
www.slc.co.uk

UKCISA: UK Council for International Student Affairs
1st Floor
3–5 Islington High Street
London N1 9LQ
Advice line for students: 020 7788 9214 (Mon–Fri, 1–4pm)
www.ukcisa.org.uk

UKCISA provides advice and information to international students studying in the UK, and to staff who work with them.

Appendix 3
Abbreviations used in the notes

AAC	Administrative Appeals Chamber
AACR	Administrative Appeals Chamber Reports
Art(s)	Article(s)
EWCA Civ	England and Wales Court of Appeal (Civil Division)
NICA	Northern Ireland Court of Appeal
para(s)	paragraph(s)
reg(s)	regulation(s)
s(s)	section(s)
Sch(s)	Schedule(s)
UKUT	United Kingdom Upper Tribunal
Vol	volume

Acts of Parliament

JSA 1995	Jobseekers Act 1995
LGFA 1992	Local Government Finance Act 1992
SSCBA 1992	Social Security Contributions and Benefits Act 1992
WRA 2007	Welfare Reform Act 2007
WRWA 2016	Welfare Reform and Work Act 2016

Regulations

Each set of regulations has a statutory instrument (SI) number and a date. You ask for them by giving their date and number.

C(LC)SSB(S) Regs	The Children (Leaving Care) Social Security Benefits (Scotland) Regulations 2004 No.747
CB Regs	The Child Benefit (General) Regulations 2006 No.223
CT(D)(S)CAO	The Council Tax (Discounts) (Scotland) Consolidation and Amendment Order 2003 No.176

Appendix 3: Abbreviations used in the notes

CTC Regs	The Child Tax Credit Regulations 2002 No.2007
CTR(S) Regs	The Council Tax Reduction (Scotland) Regulations 2012 No.303
ESA Regs	The Employment and Support Allowance Regulations 2008 No.794
ESA(TP) Regs	The Employment and Support Allowance (Transitional Provisions) Regulations 2008 No.795
HB Regs	The Housing Benefit Regulations 2006 No.213
IS Regs	The Income Support (General) Regulations 1987 No.1967
JSA Regs	The Jobseeker's Allowance Regulations 1996 No.207
JSA Regs 2013	The Jobseeker's Allowance Regulations 2013 No.378
LMI Regs	The Loans for Mortgage Interest Regulations 2017 No.725
NHS(TERC)(S) Regs	The National Health Service (Travelling Expenses and Remission of Charges) (Scotland) (No.2) Regulations 2003 No.460
SS(ICA) Regs	The Social Security (Invalid Care Allowance) Regulations 1976 No.409
TC(DCI) Regs	The Tax Credits (Definition and Calculation of Income) Regulations 2002 No.2006
UC Regs	The Universal Credit Regulations 2013 No.376

Other information

ADM	Advice for Decision Making
DMG	Decision Makers' Guide
GM	Housing Benefit/Council Tax Benefit Guidance Manual

References like CIS/142/1990 and R(JSA) 2/02 are references to commissioners' decisions.

References like *AD v SSWP* [2009] UKUT 46 (AAC) are references to decisions of the Upper Tribunal.

Index

How to use this Index

Entries against the bold headings direct you to the general information on the subject, or where the subject is covered most fully. Sub-entries are listed alphabetically and direct you to specific aspects of the subject.

CA	Carer's allowance	I-ESA	Income-related employment and support allowance
C-ESA	Contributory employment and support allowance	I-JSA	Income-based jobseeker's allowance
C-JSA	Contribution-based jobseeker's allowance	JSA	Jobseeker's allowance
CTC	Child tax credit	NI	National insurance
DLA	Disability living allowance	PIP	Personal independence payment
ESA	Employment and support allowance	UC	Universal credit
HB	Housing benefit	WTC	Working tax credit
IS	Income support		

16/17-year-olds
 child benefit 9
 free dental treatment 31
 IS 53, 62
 JSA 73
 UC 91
16-19-year-olds
 child benefit 9
 council tax 176
 education maintenance allowance 125
 estrangement from parents 53
 health benefits 32
 IS 52, 53
 JSA 69
 UC 90
16-21-year-olds
 HB 39
19 or over
 ESA 22
 HB 38
 health benefits 32
 IS 55
 JSA 70

A
academic years 146
actively seeking work
 JSA 73, 74
additional support needs for learning allowance 126
 treatment as income
  health benefits 167
  means-tested benefits 143
  tax credits 162
  UC 135

adoption
 benefits 80
advanced education
 definition 53
 full-time 55
 see also: higher education
allied healthcare students 121
amount of benefit
 CA 5
 child benefit 12
 CTC 103
 DLA 18
 ESA 24
  C-ESA 25
  I-ESA 25
 HB 43
 IS 60
 JSA 75
  C-JSA 75
  I-JSA 76
 MA 83
 PIP 87
 SMP/SAP/SPP/SSPP 83
 UC 93
 WTC 110
appeals
 see: challenging a decision
applicable amount
 ESA 26
 HB 46
 IS 61
 JSA 76
articulating students
 council tax 178

199

Index
asylum seekers – challenging a decision

asylum seekers
  health benefits 32
available for work
  JSA 72, 74

B
backdating
  CTC 104, 105
  HB 48
  IS 64
  JSA 77
  WTC 112
bedroom tax
  HB 44
  UC 96
benefit cap 49, 98
  CA 6
  child benefit 13
  CTC 106
  DLA 19
  ESA 30
  HB 49
  IS 66
  JSA 78
  MA 84
  PIP 88
  SMP/SAP/SPP/SSPP 84
  UC 98
  WTC 113
benefit week 147
Best Start foods 115
  qualifying benefits 115
Best Start grants 114
  challenging a decision 117
  claims 115
  early learning payment 114
  pregnancy and baby payment 114
  qualifying benefits 115
  school age payment 114
budgeting loans 116
  challenging a decision 117
bursary maintenance allowance 125
  treatment as income
    health benefits 167
    means-tested benefits 143
    tax credits 162
    UC 135

C
capital
  council tax reduction 181
  ESA 25
  HB 43
  health benefits 33, 171
  IS 60
  JSA 75
  lump-sum payments
    health benefits 169
    means-tested benefits 153
  means-tested benefits 157

  tax credits 164, 165
  UC 93, 138
care component
  DLA 15
care experienced accommodation grant 124
  treatment as income
    health benefits 168
    means-tested benefits 142
    tax credits 162
    UC 135
care experienced students' bursary 123, 126
  treatment as income
    health benefits 167, 168
    means-tested benefits 142, 143
    tax credits 162
    UC 135
care leavers
  care experienced accommodation grant 124
  care experienced students' bursary 123, 126
  health benefits 32
  IS 53
  JSA 74
carer element
  CA 6
  UC 95
carer premium
  CA 6
  ESA 28
  IS 63
carer's allowance 3
  amount 5
  challenging a decision 5
  claiming 5
  eligible students 4
  entitlement conditions 5
  entitlement to other benefits 6
  entitlement to WTC 6
  full-time students 4
  part-time students 4
  payment 5
carer's allowance supplement 7
  amount 7
carers
  available for work
    JSA 74
  benefits of person cared for 6
  CA 3
  carer element of UC 95
  IS 59
  time out from course 4, 188
  UC 93
challenging a decision
  Best Start grants 117
  CA 5
  child benefit 12
  CTC 106
  DLA 18
  ESA 29
  funeral support payments 117

Index
challenging a decision – council tax

HB 48
health benefits 36
IS 65
JSA 77
MA 83
PIP 88
SMP/SAP/SPP/SSPP 83
UC 98
WTC 113
change of circumstances
 CTC 105, 161
 WTC 112, 161
charitable payments 129
 treatment as income
  health benefits 170
  means-tested benefits 154
child benefit 8
 amount 12
 challenging a decision 12
 claiming 12
 eligible students 8
 entitlement to other benefits and tax credits 13
 extension period 10
 payment 12
 terminal date 11
 treatment as income
  health benefits 171
  means-tested benefits 156
  tax credits 107, 164
  UC 138
child element
 CTC 103
 UC 94
child support
 treatment as income
  means-tested benefits 156
  tax credits 165
child tax credit 101
 amount 103
 benefits treated as income 163
 calculation 103
 challenging a decision 106
 child in further education 102
 child in higher education 102
 claiming 105
 earnings 163
 eligible students 102
 entitlement to other benefits 106
 income 160
 income threshold 104
 maximum CTC 103
 overpayments 106, 161
 passport to other benefits 107
 payment 105
 treatment as income
  health benefits 171
  means-tested benefits 106, 156
 treatment of student support 162
 working out income 160

childcare
 childcare fund 124, 127
 disregarded earnings 155
 lone parents' childcare grant 124, 127
childcare allowance
 treatment as income
  health benefits 168
  means-tested benefits 143
  UC 135
childcare element
 UC 96
 WTC 111
childcare fund 124, 127
 treatment as income
  health benefits 169
  means-tested benefits 153
  tax credits 162
  UC 134, 135
children
 definition of a child
  child benefit 9
  CTC 102
  DLA 18
  UC 94
claimant commitment
 JSA 74
 UC 93
claims
 Best Start grants 115
 CA 5
 child benefit 12
 council tax reduction 181
 CTC 105
 DLA 18
 ESA 29
 HB 48
 health benefits 35
 IS 64
 JSA 77
 MA 83
 PIP 87
 SMP/SAP/SPP/SSPP 83
 UC 97
 WTC 112
community care grants 116
components
 ESA 28
 HB 47
 PIP
  daily living component 86
  mobility component 87
council tax 175
 council tax reduction 180
 definition of student 176
 disability reduction 180
 discounts 180
 exempt dwellings 178
 liability 179
 second adult rebate 181
 who pays 176

201

Index
council tax reduction – eligible rent

council tax reduction 180
  capital 181
  claiming 181
  eligible students 181
couples
  council tax 180
  HB 39
  IS 57
  JSA 71, 76, 77
  personal allowances 62
  student couples 187
crisis grants 117

D
daily living component
  PIP 86
dental treatment
  free checks 31
  free treatment
    eligible groups 32
    qualifying benefits 32
dependants' allowance 126, 128
  treatment as income
    health benefits 167, 168
    means-tested benefits 143
    UC 135
dependants' grant 123
  treatment as income
    health benefits 168
    means-tested benefits 143
    tax credits 162
    UC 134
direct entry students
  council tax 178
disability assistance for children and young people 15
disability living allowance 14
  amount 18
  care component 15
  challenging a decision 18
  claiming 18
  eligible students 15
  entitlement to other benefits and tax credits 19
  limited capability for work 23
  mobility component 17
  payment 18
  transferring to PIP 85
disability premium
  HB 39
  IS 63
  JSA 76
disabled child element
  CTC 103
disabled students
  available for work
    JSA 74
  council tax disability reduction 180
  DLA 14
  ESA 20
    C-ESA 21

    I-ESA 21
  HB 39
  PIP 85
  UC 93, 95
  WTC 109
disabled students' allowance 124, 129
  treatment as income
    health benefits 168
    means-tested benefits 142, 143
    tax credits 162
    UC 134, 135
disabled worker element
  WTC 111
discretionary funds 124
  treatment as income
    health benefits 169
    means-tested benefits 153
    tax credits 162
    UC 134, 135
discretionary housing payments
  HB 44
  UC 96
disregards
  benefits disregarded
    health benefits 170
    means-tested benefits 156
    tax credits 163
    UC 138
  earnings disregarded
    health benefits 170
    means-tested benefits 155
    tax credits 163
    UC 137
  student support disregarded
    health benefits 167
    means-tested benefits 142, 143, 146
    tax credits 162
    UC 134
  tax credits disregarded
    health benefits 170
    means-tested benefits 156

E
early learning payment 114
earnings
  treatment of earnings
    health benefits 170
    means-tested benefits 155
    tax credits 163
    UC 137
education maintenance allowance 125
  treatment as income
    health benefits 167
    means-tested benefits 143
    tax credits 162
    UC 135
educational trusts 129
eligible rent
  HB 42

Index
employment and support allowance – higher education

employment and support allowance 20
  amount 24
    C-ESA 25
    I-ESA 25
  benefits and tax credits treated as income 156
  calculating income 141
  calculation 25
  capital 25, 157
  challenging a decision 29
  claiming 29
  contributory ESA 20
  eligible students 21
    C-ESA 21
    I-ESA 21
  entitlement to other benefits and tax credits 29
  housing costs 28
  income 140
  income-related ESA 20
    new claims 20
  limited capability for work 23
  NI conditions 21
  passport to other benefits 30
  support component 28
  time out from studies 185
  work-related activity component 28
enhanced disability premium
  ESA 28
  IS 63
estrangement from parents
  IS 53, 58
  UC 91

F
family element 103
foster parents
  single foster parents
    IS 57
    UC 91
free school lunches
  ESA 30
  IS 66
  JSA 78
  tax credits 107
  UC 99
fuel costs
  HB 43
full-time students
  CA 4
  child benefit 9
  council tax reduction 181
  CTC 102
  DLA 15
  ESA
    I-ESA 21, 22
  HB 38
  ill health 184
  IS 55
    19 or over 55
    under 19 58

  JSA 70
    19 or over 70
    under 19 71
  PIP 87
  pregnancy 80, 187
  student support
    further education 124
    higher education 121
  WTC 109
funeral support payments 115
  challenging a decision 117
  qualifying benefits 116
further education
  16-21-year-olds
    HB 39
  19 or over
    IS 55
    JSA 70, 71
  council tax
    20 or over 177
    under 20 176
  student support
    full-time students 124
    part-time students 127
  student support treatment as income
    health benefits 167
    means-tested benefits 143, 152
    tax credits 162
    UC 134
  under 20
    CTC 102
    IS 52
    JSA 69
further education discretionary fund 127
  treatment as income
    health benefits 169
    means-tested benefits 153
    tax credits 162
    UC 135

G
glasses
  free checks 31
  vouchers for glasses and contact lenses 33

H
halls of residence 42
health benefits 31
  benefits treated as income 170
  capital 171
  challenging a decision 36
  claiming 35
  earnings 170
  eligible students 31
  income 166
  low income scheme 33
  student support treatment as income 167
  working out income 166
higher education
  19 or over
    HB 38

Index
higher education – income support

IS 55
JSA 70
council tax 177
student support
  full-time students 121
  part-time students 127
student support treatment as income
  health benefits 167
  means-tested benefits 142, 152
  tax credits 162
  UC 134
under 19
  IS 58
  JSA 71
Higher National Certificate 121
Higher National Diploma 121
home
  HB 41
  two homes
    HB 41
    IS 64
hospital
  fares to hospital 32, 33
housing benefit 37
  amount 43
  benefit cap 49
  benefits and tax credits treated as income 156
  calculating income 141
  calculation 43
  capital 43, 157
  challenging a decision 48
  claiming 48
  discretionary housing payments 44
  eligible accommodation 42
  eligible rent 42
  eligible students 38
  entitlement conditions 40
  entitlement to other benefits and tax credits 49
  full-time students 38
  income 140
  local housing allowance 44
  lone parents 39
  maximum rent 43
  new claims 37
  non-dependant deductions 45
  part-time students 40
  passport to other benefits 49
  payment 48
  payment on account 48
  people living with you 45
  rent restrictions 43
  summer vacation 41
  who can claim 39
housing costs
  met by ESA 28
  met by IS 64
  met by JSA 76
  met by UC 95

I
incapacity for work
  HB 39
income
  benefits and tax credits treated as income
    health benefits 170
    means-tested benefits 156
    tax credits 163
    UC 138
  change in income
    tax credits 161
  earnings
    health benefits 170
    means-tested benefits 155
    tax credits 163
    UC 137
  ESA 140
  HB 140
  health benefits 33, 166
  IS 140
  JSA 140
  maintenance
    health benefits 171
    means-tested benefits 156
    tax credits 165
  property income
    tax credits 165
  regular payments
    health benefits 169
    means-tested benefits 154
  tax credits 160
  UC 133
  weekly income 146
  working out income
    health benefits 166
    means-tested benefits 141
    tax credits 160
    UC 133
income support 51
  amount 60
  benefits and tax credits treated as income 156
  calculating income 141
  calculation 60
  capital 60, 157
  challenging a decision 65
  claiming 64
  eligible students 52
  entitlement conditions 60
  entitlement to other benefits and tax credits 65
  full-time students 55
  housing costs 64
  income 140
  lone parents 51, 57
  new claims 51
  part-time students 58
  passport to other benefits 66
  payment 65
  refusal of claim 65

Index
income support – mortgage interest loan

relevant education 52
single foster parents 57
income threshold
  CTC 104
  WTC 112
independent students' bursary 123
  treatment as income
    health benefits 167
    means-tested benefits 142
    tax credits 162
    UC 134

J
jobseeker's allowance 68
  actively seeking work 73, 74
  amount 75
    C-JSA 75
    I-JSA 76
  available for work 72, 74
  benefits and tax credits treated as income 156
  calculating income 141
  capital 75, 157
  challenging a decision 77
  claiming 77
  contribution-based JSA 68
  eligible students 69
  entitlement conditions 74
    C-JSA 75
    I-JSA 75
  entitlement to other benefits and tax credits 78
  full-time students 70
  housing costs 76
  income 140
  income-based JSA 68
    new claims 69
  lone parents studying full time 71
  part-time students 71
  passport to other benefits 78
  relevant education 69
  summer vacations 71

L
limited capability for work
  ESA 23
  HB 39
  time out from studies 185
  UC 91, 95
living away from home
  bursary maintenance allowance 126
loan for mortgage interest
  see: mortgage interest loan
local housing allowance
  HB 44
  UC 96
lone parent element 111
lone parents
  benefits 187
  childcare grant 124, 127
  earnings disregards

means-tested benefits 155
  HB 39
  IS 51, 57
  JSA 71
  nursing and midwifery students 129
  personal allowances
    IS 62
    UC 93
lone parents' childcare grant 124, 127
  treatment as income
    health benefits 167, 168
    means-tested benefits 142, 143
    tax credits 162
    UC 134, 135
lone parents' grant 123
  treatment as income
    health benefits 168
    means-tested benefits 142
    tax credits 162
    UC 134
low income
  health benefits 33
lump-sum payments
  health benefits 169
  means-tested benefits 153

M
maintenance
  treatment as income
    health benefits 171
    means-tested benefits 156
    tax credits 165
maternity
  benefits 80, 187
  Best Start foods 115
  Best Start grants 114
  health benefits 32
  time out from studies 187
maternity allowance 81
  amount 83
  challenging a decision 83
  claiming 83
  entitlement conditions 81
  entitlement to other benefits and tax credits 84
maximum rent
  HB 43
meal charges
  HB 43
midwifery students
  student support 128
  student support treatment as income 143
mobility component
  DLA 17
  PIP 87
modular courses
  IS 56
mortgage interest loan
  ESA 28
  IS 64
  UC 95

Index
mortgage interest loan – postgraduate students

N
national insurance contributions
  C-ESA 21
  C-JSA 75
NHS low income scheme 166
non-advanced education
  child benefit 9, 10
  CTC 102
  definition 53
  ESA 22
  full-time 55
  IS 52
  JSA 69, 70
  part-time 59
  see also: further education
non-dependant deductions
  HB 45
nursing and midwifery bursary 128
  treatment as income
    health benefits 168
    means-tested benefits 143, 152
    tax credits 162
    UC 135
nursing students
  student support 128
  student support treatment as income 143

O
online claims
  Best Start grants 115
  C-JSA 77
  CA 5
  HB 48
  IS 64
  UC 97
orphans
  IS 53
overlapping benefits
  CA 6
overpayments
  tax credits 106, 161

P
parents
  benefits 80
  child benefit 8
  CTC 101
  fathers 187
  living apart from parents
    IS 53, 58
    UC 91
  student couples 187
    HB 39
    IS 57
    JSA 77
  working hours
    WTC 109
part-time students
  CA 4
  child benefit 9
  council tax reduction 181
  CTC 102
  DLA 15
  ESA
    I-ESA 21
  HB 40
  ill health 186
  IS 58
  JSA 70, 71
  PIP 87
  pregnancy 80, 187
  student support
    further education 127
    higher education 127
  WTC 109
passported benefits
  ESA 30
  HB 49
  IS 66
  JSA 78
  tax credits 107
  UC 99
paternity
  benefits 80
  time out from studies 187
payment on account
  HB 48
pension credit
  capital 157
  HB 39
pensioner premium
  ESA 27
  IS 63
personal allowances
  ESA 27
  HB 46
  IS 62
  JSA 76
personal independence payment 85
  amount 87
  challenging a decision 88
  claiming 87
  daily living component 86
  eligible students 86
  entitlement to other benefits and tax
    credits 88
  full-time students 87
  limited capability for work 23
  mobility component 87
  part-time students 87
  payment 88
  time out from studies 185
plus one year 122
postgraduate students
  IS 56
  JSA 70
  student support 128
  student support treatment as income
    health benefits 168
    means-tested benefits 143, 153
    tax credits 162
    UC 134

pregnancy
  benefits 80, 187
  Best Start foods 115
  Best Start grants 114
  health benefits 32
  time out from studies 187
pregnancy and baby payment 114
premiums
  ESA 27
  HB 46
  IS 63
  JSA 76
prescriptions
  free 31
professional and career development loans
  treatment as income
    health benefits 170
    means-tested benefits 154
    tax credits 162
    UC 137
Professional Graduate Diploma in Education 121
property
  treatment of income
    tax credits 165

Q
qualifying young person
  child benefit 9
  ESA 22
  UC 90

R
re-sitting exams 188
receiving education
  UC 90
reconsideration
  see: challenging a decision
refugees
  IS 58
regular payments
  health benefits 169
  means-tested benefits 154
relevant education
  course ends 54
  definition
    IS 52
    JSA 69
  IS 52
  JSA 69
rent
  eligible rent
    HB 42
    HB 37
  liable for rent
    HB 40
    UC 95
  maximum rent
    HB 43
  two homes

HB 41
UC 95
rent restrictions
  private tenants
    HB 44
    UC 96
  social sector tenants
    HB 44
    UC 96

S
sanctions
  JSA 73
  UC 92
sandwich course
  IS 56
scholarships 129
school age payment 114
Scottish Welfare Fund 116
  challenging a decision 117
SDS Individual Training Accounts 129
  treatment as income
    means-tested benefits 155
    UC 137
second adult rebate 181
self-employment
  tax credits 164
service charges
  HB 44
severe disability element
  WTC 111
severe disability premium
  ESA 28
  HB 39
  IS 63
severely disabled child element
  CTC 103
sickness
  ESA 20
  full-time students 184
  part-time students 186
  suspension of loan 186
  time out from studies 184
  UC 95
single parents' allowance
  treatment as income
    health benefits 168
    means-tested benefits 143
    UC 135
single room rent
  HB 44
social fund
  budgeting loans 116
sponsorship 129
statutory adoption pay 81
  amount 83
  challenging a decision 83
  claiming 83
  entitlement conditions 82
  entitlement to other benefits and tax credits 84

207

Index
statutory adoption pay – universal credit

treatment as income
 tax credits 163
statutory maternity pay 80
 amount 83
 challenging a decision 83
 claiming 83
 entitlement conditions 81
 entitlement to other benefits and tax credits 84
 treatment as income
  tax credits 163
statutory paternity pay 81
 amount 83
 challenging a decision 83
 claiming 83
 entitlement conditions 82
 entitlement to other benefits and tax credits 84
 treatment as income
  tax credits 163
statutory shared parental pay 81
 amount 83
 challenging a decision 83
 claiming 83
 entitlement conditions 82
 entitlement to other benefits and tax credits 84
 treatment as income
  tax credits 163
statutory sick pay
 treatment as income
  tax credits 163
student grants
 calculating weekly income 151
 treatment as income
  health benefits 167
  means-tested benefits 142
  tax credits 162
  UC 135
student loans 122
 calculating weekly income 146
 suspended due to ill health 186
 treatment as income
  health benefits 167, 168
  means-tested benefits 145
  tax credits 162
  UC 134
student support 121
 further education
  full-time students 124
  part-time students 127
 higher education
  full-time students 121
  part-time students 127
 ill health 186
 nursing and midwifery students 128
 postgraduates 128
 treatment as income
  health benefits 167
  means-tested benefits 142
  tax credits 162

UC 134
 tuition fees 122
study expenses allowance 126
 treatment as income
  health benefits 167
  means-tested benefits 143
  tax credits 162
  UC 135

T
Tax Credit Helpline 105
tax credits
 income 160
 see also: child tax credit, working tax credit
term-time accommodation 41
time out from studies 184
 carers 4, 188
 ill health 184
 pregnancy 187
travel expenses 122
travel expenses allowance 126
 treatment as income
  health benefits 167, 168
  means-tested benefits 142, 143
  tax credits 162
  UC 134, 135
tuition fees 122
 part-time fee grant 127
 treatment as income
  health benefits 168
  means-tested benefits 142
  tax credits 162
  UC 134, 135
two homes
 HB 41
 IS 64

U
underpayments
 tax credits 161
universal credit 89
 amount 93
 assessment periods 136
 benefit cap 98
 benefits treated as income 138
 budgeting advance 98
 calculating income 133
 calculation 93
 capital 138
 carer element 95
 challenging a decision 98
 child element 94
 childcare element 96
 claiming 97
 disability 95
 discretionary housing payments 96
 eligible students 90
 entitlement conditions 93
 entitlement to other benefits 98
 housing costs element 95

208

non-dependants 95
illness 95
income 133
local housing allowance 96
maximum amount 94
passport to other benefits 99
payment 97
standard allowance 94
who can claim 90
work-related requirements 92

young students' bursary 123
treatment as income
health benefits 167
means-tested benefits 142, 145
tax credits 162
UC 134

V
vacations
HB 41
JSA 71
vouchers
glasses and contact lenses
eligible groups 33
qualifying benefits 32

W
war pensioners
health benefits 32
water charges
HB 43
work capability assessment 23
work-focused interviews 23
work-related requirements
UC 92
working tax credit 108
amount 110
benefits treated as income 163
calculation 110
challenging a decision 113
claiming 112
earnings 163
eligible students 109
entitlement to other benefits 113
income 160
income threshold 110, 112
maximum WTC 111
new claims 112
overpayments 106, 161
passport to other benefits 107
payment 112
treatment as income
health benefits 171
means-tested benefits 106, 156
treatment of student support 162
working hours 109
working out income 160

Y
young carer grant 7
amount 7
young person
qualifying young person
child benefit 9
ESA 22